Cordon Bleu

Memorable
Meals

Cordon Bleu

Memorable Meals

Macdonald and Jane's
London

Macdonald and Jane's
London

Published by
Macdonald and Jane's Publishers Ltd
Paulton House
8 Shepherdess Walk
London N1

Copyright B.P.C. Publishing Ltd., 1972

This impression 1977

Designed by Melvin Kyte
Printed by Waterlow (Dunstable) Ltd

These recipes have been adapted from the Cordon Bleu Cookery Course
published by Purnell in association with the London Cordon Bleu Cookery
School
Principal: Rosemary Hume; Co-Principal: Muriel Downes

Contents

Introduction

Be honest — when does your cooking matter most? Of course, it's when you are entertaining. And that, too, is when it is most difficult. For when you have guests coming there is no time to nurse a complicated dish to perfection — you have other dishes to attend to, the table to set, yourself to groom and then you have to be cool and collected to talk to your guests over drinks.

We hope this book will help you perfect the art of producing truly 'memorable meals'. The dishes are co-ordinated to please the most discerning palate and at the same time to relieve the cook of too much juggling during preparation. A happy hostess — or host — makes for a successful party and even without practice you can become a confident party cook if you follow the special timetables we have drawn up to guide you through the order of preparation for each menu. If you have help in the kitchen you can be more flexible in your timing of last minute cooking.

Each menu we have given is for a three-course meal, and we have usually suggested alternatives for either the starter or the dessert. So if your main course is a wild success the first time, and your guests demand a repeat performance, you can give it some variation on the next occasion and still make full use of our helpful timetable.

No meal is complete without wine and, while your choice will depend largely on your taste, a dish made with fine ingredients, such as sole or fillet of beef, deserves a fine wine. If you are not sure what to choose, ask your wine merchant's advice — tell him what you are eating and what you wish to pay and follow his guidance. It is also a good idea to make a note with the recipe if you particularly enjoyed the wine you drank with it.

This series of **Cordon Bleu Cookery Books** is designed to help you enjoy your cooking. There are certain basic rules without which no cook can succeed, and we have included those that are relevant to our menus; but the main part of this book aims to take the chore out of cooking for entertaining and make it fun. Cordon Bleu cooking methods are basically French, and the French don't take short cuts — our co-ordinated menus enable you to combine these traditional cooking methods with efficient use of the time available, so that you produce a superb meal, on time and unflustered.

Rosemary Hume
Muriel Downes

You will find that **cooking times** given in the individual recipes in this book have sometimes been adapted in the timetables to help you when cooking and serving the menus as three-course meals.

Quantities given are for 4 servings. Spoon measures are level unless otherwise stated.

Menu 1 Beef

Starter : Iced curry soup
Alternative : Sole à l'indienne

Main course : Braised fillet of beef chasseur

Dessert : Boîte au chocolat aux fruits

TIMETABLE

Day before
Make demi-glace sauce for
beef dish.
Make sponge cake and
chocolate squares.
Make stock for soup (or
mayonnaise for fish).

Morning
Make soup, and curry
foundation for cream
topping (or cook fish and
rice and make curry cream
sauce).
Wash and trim mushrooms.
Prepare the vegetables.
Tie the beef.
Put soup, when cold, in
covered container to chill in
refrigerator.

Assemble ingredients and
equipment for final cooking
from 6.30 for dinner
around 8 pm.

Order of work

6.30 Finish off cake.
(Make rice mixture and
dish up fish.)

7.10 Start cooking beef.

7.25 Put beef in oven.

7.30 Start cooking potatoes
and green vegetable
of your choice.
Sauté mushrooms and
shallot and reduce wine;
add tomato purée.
Finish off cream
topping for soup.
Dish up vegetables.

7.55 Take up beef and keep
warm.
Strain sauce, add it to
mushroom mixture and
keep warm.

8.00 Serve first course.
Carve beef between
courses and dish up.

Iced curry soup

1 oz butter
4 shallots, or 1 medium-size
   onion (finely chopped)
1 tablespoon curry paste
1 oz flour
1¾ pints chicken, or well-
   flavoured vegetable, stock
   (see pages 151, 158)
strip of lemon rind
1 bayleaf
¼ pint boiling water
1 tablespoon ground almonds
1 tablespoon desiccated coconut
1 dessertspoon arrowroot
1 tablespoon cold stock, or water

For cream topping
1 glass port
1 teaspoon curry powder
1 dessertspoon apricot jam, or
   purée of fresh, or dried,
   apricots
4 tablespoons double cream

Method

Melt three-quarters of the butter, add the shallot (or onion) and cook it slowly until just turning colour, then add the curry paste and a dusting of the flour; fry gently for 4-5 minutes. Stir in the remainder of the butter and when it has melted blend in the rest of the flour and the stock; bring to the boil. Add the lemon rind and bayleaf and simmer for 20 minutes. Strain the liquid and return it to the rinsed pan; continue simmering for 10-15 minutes.

Meanwhile pour the boiling water over the almonds and coconut and leave them to soak for 30 minutes, then squeeze mixture in a piece of muslin and add the 'milk' obtained to the soup. Mix the arrowroot with the tablespoon of cold stock (or water), add it to the pan and reboil. Strain soup again, allow it to cool and then chill.

To make the cream topping: mix the port and curry powder together and simmer until reduced to half quantity. Leave this until cold, then mix in the jam (or purée) and squeeze the mixture in a piece of muslin; reserve the liquid. Lightly whip the cream and stir in the 'essence' from the wine and curry mixture. Serve the soup with a spoonful of this cream in each soup cup.

The liquid from the wine, curry and jam mixture is stirred into whipped cream to make the topping

Iced curry soup, served in cups with a spoonful of cream topping in each

Braised fillet of beef chasseur

2 lb fillet of beef
2 large carrots
1 large onion
1 tablespoon beef dripping, or oil
½ lb mushrooms
½ oz butter
1 shallot (finely chopped)
1 wineglass white wine
1 teaspoon tomato purée

For demi-glace sauce
2 tablespoons oil
2 tablespoons finely diced onion, carrot and celery
¾ oz flour
1 pint jellied bone stock
1 teaspoon tomato purée
a few mushroom peelings
bouquet garni
salt and pepper

Method

First prepare the demi-glace sauce, which may be done the day before if wished. Cook the vegetables in the oil until soft, then add the flour; continue cooking very slowly to a good russet-brown. Allow mixture to cool a little, then pour on three-quarters of the stock; return pan to the heat and stir until boiling. Add the remaining ingredients and leave to simmer very gently for about 30 minutes. Add half the reserved stock, bring to the boil and skim; simmer for 5 minutes. Repeat this process, then strain the sauce; return it to the rinsed pan, adjust the seasoning and continue simmering for 5-10 minutes, skimming if necessary.

Set the oven at 350°F or Mark 4.

Tie the beef at regular intervals to keep it a good shape and to prevent it curling when being browned. Slice the onion and carrots into rounds. Take a heavy flameproof casserole, heat the dripping and, when it is smoking, put in the fillet and brown it on all sides; take meat out of pan, reduce the heat and add the onion and carrot. Cover the pan and cook gently for about 10 minutes to allow the vegetables to absorb the dripping and begin to brown. Replace the meat and pour the demi-glace sauce over it; cover with a paper and tight-fitting lid and bring to the boil. Put into a pre-set moderate oven for 20 minutes if you like your beef pink in the centre, 30 minutes if you like your beef well done.

Meanwhile wash and trim the mushrooms and sauté them quickly in the butter; add the shallot, cook for 1 minute, then pour on the wine and reduce it by half. Stir in the tomato purée. Take up the beef; slice it and arrange on the hot serving dish. Strain the sauce from the meat on to the mushroom mixture and boil up well; taste for seasoning. Lift the mushrooms from the sauce with a draining spoon, place at each side of the dish and then moisten the meat with 2-3 tablespoons of the sauce. Serve with new potatoes cooked in butter, the remainder of the sauce in a sauce boat, and a green vegetable of your choice.

Boîte au chocolat aux fruits

3 eggs
4½ oz caster sugar
1 tablespoon boiling water
3 oz plain flour (sifted with pinch of salt)

To finish
3 oz plain block chocolate
2-3 tablespoons rum, or kirsch, or Grand
   Marnier
½ lb raspberries, or strawberries, or 2-3
   fresh peaches (sliced)
caster sugar (to sweeten fruit)
¼-½ pint double cream (whipped)

8-inch square cake tin

Method

Set the oven at 350°F or Mark 4. Grease
and flour the cake tin.

Separate the eggs. Beat the yolks
thoroughly with half the sugar and the
boiling water in a bowl over hot water.
When mixture is thick and mousse-like,
remove bowl from the heat.

Whisk the whites stiffly, then whisk in the
rest of the sugar; cut and fold this into the
yolk mixture with the sifted flour and salt.
Turn mixture at once into prepared tin; bake
for about 25 minutes in a pre-set moderate
oven. Turn cake out and cool.

Meanwhile break up the chocolate and
melt it over very gentle heat, but do not
allow the chocolate itself to reach more
than blood heat (98°F). Spread this evenly
and moderately thickly over a large square
of greaseproof paper and, when just set,
mark into small squares (1¾ inches) with a
sharp knife. Leave in a cool airy room to
harden completely.

Sprinkle the cake well with the rum (or
liqueur) and prepare the fruit. Then sugar
the fruit and leave to stand for a short time.
Spread the sides of the cake with the
whipped cream. Peel the chocolate squares
off the paper and press them round the sides
of the cake, slightly overlapping. Top edge of
squares should come above top of cake. Fill
cake with fruit and pile more cream on top.

When hard, chocolate squares are removed from paper with palette knife

Sugared raspberries are placed on top of cake before cream is added

Sole à l'indienne

2 filleted soles
  (each weighing 1¼ lb)
salt
6 peppercorns
juice of ½ lemon
1 lemon (to garnish)
paprika pepper (to garnish)

For curry cream sauce

1 tablespoon chopped onion
2 tablespoons oil
1 clove of garlic (chopped)
1 dessertspoon curry powder

½ pint tomato juice
salt and pepper
2-3 slices of lemon
1 tablespoon apricot jam
½ pint mayonnaise (see page 154)

For rice mixture

4 oz long grain rice
4 oz firm button mushrooms
squeeze of lemon juice
salt and pepper
4 oz prawns (shelled)
4 tablespoons French dressing (see
  page 152)

Method

Trim, wash and dry the fillets. Fold them and place in a buttered ovenproof dish; season with salt, lay the peppercorns on one side and squeeze lemon juice over the fillets. Cover with a buttered paper and poach in a very moderate oven, pre-set at 350°F or Mark 4, for 8-10 minutes. Cool and drain.

To make curry cream sauce: soften the onion in the oil with the chopped garlic. Add the curry powder and cook for a few minutes, then add the tomato juice. Simmer for 7-10 minutes, then add seasoning and the lemon slices. Stir in the jam and strain the liquid; cool it slightly, add the mayonnaise and adjust seasoning.

Cook the rice in boiling salted water for about 12 minutes; drain, refresh and dry it. Trim the mushrooms, wash them quickly in salted water, then slice them and cook quickly for 1 minute with a squeeze of lemon and salt and pepper to taste; allow to cool. Mix the rice, prawns and mushrooms together; moisten with the French dressing and spoon on to the serving dish.

Arrange the fillets of fish on the rice and coat them with the sauce. Garnish each fillet with a thin slice of lemon dusted with paprika. Serve remaining sauce separately.

Menu 2 Beef

Starter : Eggs Jacqueline
Alternative : Aubergine with crab

Main course : Médaillons de boeuf

Dessert : Timbale Orta

TIMETABLE

Day before
Roast the fillet of beef.
Stone and cook the cherries,
cover and keep in a cool place.
Hardboil the eggs ; leave the
shells on. If using home-made
aspic, prepare it.

Morning
Make up powdered aspic, using
sherry for some of the liquid.
Cook mushrooms for garnish.
Cut beef and ham, spread
creamed pâté on beef rounds
and cover with ham ; coat with
aspic.
Cook potatoes and beans for
salads. Prepare dressings.
Measure ingredients for pudding and sauce ; prepare tin.
Fill eggs and cook asparagus,
arrange them with the prawns
in ovenproof dish.
(If aubergines are chosen,
prepare them and leave on
baking tray ready to brown
in oven.)

Assemble equipment for final
cooking from 6.30 for dinner
around 8pm.

Order of work

6.30 Set oven and make
sponge.

6.45 Put sponge to cook in
oven; dish up main course
and dress salads.

7.10 Put cherries into pan
ready for heating and
begin to make béchamel
sauce.
Put cherries on to heat.

7.30 Take up sponge pudding
and fill with cherries (keep
in the warming drawer
until eggs are finished) ;
set the oven at 400°F or
Mark 6 ; coat eggs with
béchamel sauce.

7.40 Put the completed egg
dish in the oven. (Put
aubergines in oven to
brown.) Assemble
ingredients, utensils and
pan ready to make
sabayon sauce just before
serving the pudding.
(This is kept in turned-off
oven after eggs are
taken out).

8.00 Serve first course.

Eggs Jacqueline

4 eggs
1½ oz butter
½ teaspoon paprika pepper
6 oz shelled prawns
salt and pepper
1 packet (about 12 oz) frozen
   asparagus
½ pint béchamel sauce (see page
   150)

To finish

1 tablespoon grated Parmesan
   cheese

Method

Hardboil the eggs and cut them in two lengthways. Sieve the yolks and place the whites in a bowl of cold water. Cream the butter with the paprika and mix with the yolks, adding 2 oz of the prawns, finely chopped. Season to taste. Cook the asparagus following the instructions on the packet, drain, refresh it with cold water to set the colour and drain again.

Prepare the béchamel sauce, season to taste and simmer for 2-3 minutes. Place the asparagus in a buttered ovenproof dish, fill the egg whites with the prawn mixture and place on the asparagus. Scatter the remaining prawns (whole) on top. Coat the filled eggs with the béchamel sauce, sprinkle with the cheese and bake in hot oven at 400°F or Mark 6 for 15-20 minutes until golden-brown.

Eggs Jacqueline make an unusual starter to a delicious summer meal

Médaillons de bœuf

1 lb fillet of beef (in the piece)
8 oz pâté de foie
2-3 oz butter (creamed)
1 truffle, or 6-8 button mushrooms
$\frac{1}{4}$ teaspoon Dijon mustard (optional)
1-2 teaspoons sherry (optional)
8 oz cooked gammon (sliced)
1$\frac{1}{2}$ pints aspic jelly (see page 150)

Method

Set oven at 400°F or Mark 7. Bard (wrap fat round) meat and tie at regular intervals with fine string. Heat 2-3 tablespoons dripping or oil in roasting tin and, when hot, take out of oven, put in fillet, baste, turn and baste again. Lift joint on to the grill pan grid or place on a wire cake rack and stand this in the tin. Roast for 30-35 minutes, basting and turning when meat is half cooked. Leave until quite cold. Work the pâté de foie with the butter and, if you are using truffle to garnish, add the trimmings (finely chopped) to flavour; if not, add the Dijon mustard and sherry.

Cut the fillet in $\frac{1}{4}$-inch thick slices; trim and cut a round of ham to fit each slice of beef. Pipe or carefully spread a layer of pâté on top of each piece of fillet and lay the slices of ham on top. Press lightly together and smooth round the edge. Lay these pieces (they should be about $\frac{1}{2}$ inch thick) in a shallow dish or tin and spoon in just enough cold, but still liquid, aspic to cover. Leave until just set, then garnish each piece with a slice of truffle, or whole cooked mushroom. (Wipe button mushrooms and cook in a little water and lemon juice for 1-2 minutes. Do not use butter or oil which would cloud the aspic.) Coat again with cold aspic and leave until set.

To serve; cut round the slices in aspic with a round or oval cutter and dish up, surrounding with the remaining aspic (chopped). Serve with potatoes dressed with vinaigrette and cooked French beans tossed in French dressing (see page 152).

Main course

Slice the roast fillet of beef and spread the slices with pâté de foie which has been mixed with butter

Having set the beef and gammon slices in aspic, garnish with truffle slices and cover with more aspic

Timbale Orta

For sponge

4 oz butter
4 oz caster sugar
grated rind and juice of $\frac{1}{4}$ orange
2 eggs (beaten)
**4 oz self-raising flour (sifted with
   a pinch of salt)**

For cherry compote

1 lb cherries
1 dessertspoon caster sugar
pinch of ground cinnamon
2 tablespoons brandy
**1-2 tablespoons redcurrant jelly
   (see page 156)**

*Timbale, or charlotte, tin (1$\frac{1}{2}$-2 pints
   capacity)*

Method

Set oven at 375°F or Mark 5.
Prepare tin by greasing and
dusting with flour.

To make the sponge: soften
butter with a wooden spoon,
add sugar and orange rind and
beat until light and fluffy. Add
eggs, a little at a time, and beat
thoroughly. Fold in the sifted
flour and add the orange juice.
Spoon mixture into the prepared
tin. Give the tin a sharp tap on
the table to settle the mixture,
then bake for about 45 minutes
in the pre-set hot oven.

Meanwhile stone the cherries
and place them in a saucepan
with the sugar and cinnamon.
Cover pan and shake over
gentle heat until the juice begins
to run. Add brandy. Continue
cooking for 10-15 minutes, then
stir in the redcurrant jelly.

Hollow out the centre of the
underside of the sponge and fill
with the hot cherries. Cut a lid
from the piece of sponge removed and place it over the
cherries before inverting sponge
on to a serving dish. (You can
save the extra pieces of sponge
and use them for Bakewell tart
or trifle.)

Serve hot with a sabayon
sauce (see recipe right), a little
poured over and around the
sponge and the rest in a sauce
boat.

Watchpoint Do not start to make
the sauce until the cherry pudding is in its serving dish.

*Spooning the hot cherry compote
into the hollowed-out sponge cake*

The timbale Orta is served hot, with a little sabayon sauce poured over it

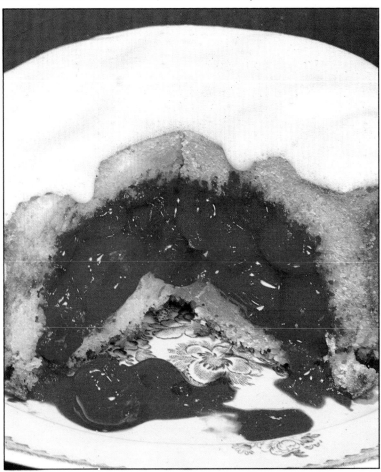

Sabayon sauce

Put 3 egg yolks, 1 tablespoon caster sugar, $\frac{1}{4}$ pint sherry and a small strip of lemon rind into a small basin and stand on a small saucepan containing a little simmering water. Whisk until sauce becomes very frothy and starts to thicken. Remove lemon rind and serve at once.

Sabayon is the French corruption of zabaione (or zabaglione), the Italian sweet which can be served as a sauce for a pudding, or on its own in a warmed glass, with Savoy fingers. In Italy this is made with Marsala or white wine instead of sherry.

Aubergine with crab

2 good-size aubergines
6-7 oz crab claw meat
salt and pepper
oil
2 medium-size onions
1 dessertspoon paprika pepper
1 tablespoon tomato purée
$\frac{1}{2}$ lb ripe tomatoes (skinned,
   seeds removed, and sliced)
$\frac{1}{2}$ teaspoon oregano
pinch of cayenne pepper, or drop
   of Tabasco sauce
2 tablespoons grated Parmesan
   and Gruyère cheese (mixed)
1-2 tablespoons melted butter

Method

Split aubergines in two length-ways, score, sprinkle with salt and leave for 30 minutes. Set oven at 350°F or Mark 4.

Wipe aubergines dry, then brown the cut surface in a little hot oil; take out, set on a baking tin and cook in pre-set moderate oven until tender (about 10 minutes).

Meanwhile slice onions and soften in 2-3 tablespoons oil; add paprika and after a few seconds add tomato purée, tomatoes, oregano and cayenne (or Tabasco). Season and cook to a rich pulp. Scoop out the pulp from the cooked aubergines, add it to the pan and continue to cook for a few minutes. Then flake the crab meat with a fork and add it to the pan. Pile this mixture into the aubergine skins, sprinkle well with cheese and melted butter and bake in quick oven (425°F or Mark 7) for 6-7 minutes to brown.

Aubergine with crab: aubergines stuffed with onion, tomato and crab meat and browned in the oven

Menu 3 Beef

Starter : Artichokes vinaigrette
Alternative : Gratin of seafood

Main course : Roast fillet of beef Dubarry

Dessert : Oranges in caramel with brandy snaps

TIMETABLE

Day before
Make brandy snaps and store
unfilled in airtight container.
Make caramel for oranges.

Morning
Cook artichokes, prepare
dressing but do not add ham.
Chop ham and keep covered
with wet greaseproof paper
to preserve colour. (Prepare
fish, put in dishes with lemon
juice. Wash and slice
mushrooms, mix with prawns
and add to fish. Prepare
white sauce for gratin, coat
fish mixture with sauce,
sprinkle with cheese and
leave for baking.) Peel and
shape potatoes. Bard and tie
meat. Shred and cook orange
rind for garnish. Cut oranges,
cover dish and put to chill.

Assemble ingredients and
equipment for final cooking
from 6.00 for dinner
around 8pm.

Order of work

6.00 Pour caramel over
oranges, garnish and put
back to chill.
Whip cream and fill the
brandy snaps.

6.15 Set oven.
Brown potatoes, drain
and then cover. Put
roasting tin with dripping /
oil in oven to heat and
potatoes on shelf below.
Put meat in fat, baste and
turn as method, return
to oven on grid.

6.30 Baste again.

7.00 Turn meat and baste.

7.15 Put cauliflower on top
shelf of the oven.
Remove potatoes, keep
in pan.

Finish artichokes and
dish up. (Put gratin
dishes on shelf under
meat.)
Baste meat again.

7.30 Remove meat from oven
and place on serving
dish. Turn oven to lowest
heat and put meat to
keep hot. (Leave gratin
dishes to keep hot.)
Make gravy, strain and
keep hot in saucepan.
Arrange cauliflower on
the serving dish.

8.00 Dish up potatoes.
Serve first course.
Carve beef between
courses.

Artichokes vinaigrette

4 globe artichokes

For vinaigrette dressing
2 shallots (finely chopped)
6 tablespoons olive oil
2-3 oz mushrooms (finely
  chopped)
3 tablespoons white wine
2 tablespoons white wine vinegar
salt and pepper
squeeze of lemon juice (optional)
1 clove of garlic (optional)
3 oz ham (thinly sliced and finely
  chopped)
1 tablespoon chopped parsley, or
  chopped mixed herbs

Method
Trim off the points and leaves of the artichokes with scissors and trim the stalk from the bottom. Plunge artichokes into boiling salted water and boil gently until a leaf can be pulled out (about 35-40 minutes). Then drain, refresh, and leave until cold.

Meanwhile prepare the dressing. Sauté the shallots slowly until just tender in 2 tablespoons of the oil, add the mushrooms and cook for 2-3 minutes. Turn into a bowl and leave until cool, then add wine, vinegar and remaining oil. Season well and add a squeeze of lemon juice if the dressing is not sharp enough. Flavour with a little garlic, if liked, and add the ham. Leave this to marinate for 15-20 minutes.

Chopped shallots, mushrooms and ham are mixed with wine, vinegar and oil to make vinaigrette dressing

After some of the centre leaves and the chokes have been removed, the dressing is spooned into artichokes

Prepare each artichoke by pulling out some of the centre leaves until the choke can be reached; carefully scrape this away with a dessertspoon. Put a spoonful of the dressing in the centre of each artichoke, set them on individual dishes and dust with the chopped parsley or herbs. Serve cold.

The artichokes, filled with special thick dressing, are served on individual plates as a first course

Roast fillet of beef Dubarry

2½-3 lb fillet of beef
piece of pork fat, or unsmoked
   bacon fat, or beef fat
   (for barding)
2-3 tablespoons oil, or beef
   dripping

For gravy
1 dessertspoon flour
½-¾ pint beef stock
salt and pepper

For garnish
1 large cauliflower
little grated cheese

For thick mornay sauce
1 oz butter
2 tablespoons flour
1 pint milk
2 oz grated cheese

Method

The garnish can be prepared ahead of time. Break the cauliflower into sprigs and cook until just tender in boiling, salted water (about 5 minutes). Drain and refresh by pouring over cold water. Press 1-2 cauliflower sprigs at a time in muslin to form balls and set them on a buttered baking sheet. Have ready the mornay sauce (see right) and coat the tiny cauliflower sprigs with this. Sprinkle with a little extra grated cheese and keep on one side.

Put the beef to roast (see method, page 20). Baste every 15 minutes and turn meat when half cooked. In a gas oven allow 15 minutes per lb and 15 minutes over (for a 3 lb or larger piece, cook 15 minutes per lb with no extra time). In an electric oven allow 10 minutes per lb with no extra time. Bake the cauliflower sprigs on the top shelf of the oven for 10-15 minutes while it is still at a roasting temperature.

Take cooked meat from oven, remove string and barding fat; keep the joint warm. Tilt the roasting tin gently and pour off the fat, take care to leave the sediment and juices undisturbed in the corner of the pan (to do this successfully use a spoon for the last of the dripping).

Dust pan very lightly with the flour, work this into the sediment and scrape down the sides of the pan. Cook over a gentle heat until well coloured. Draw

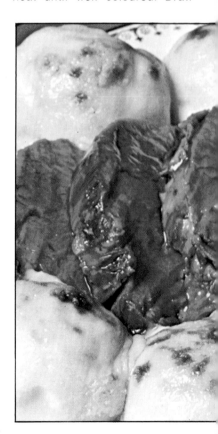

aside and blend in the stock. Stir gravy until boiling, season, and then boil hard until well-reduced and strong in flavour. Strain into a gravy boat.

Just before serving, carve the meat in the kitchen and put back on hot serving dish, spooning any juice that runs out over meat.

Watchpoint Never add these juices to the gravy.

Arrange the small cauliflower sprigs round the dish and serve with château potatoes (potatoes browned in butter and cooked, covered, in oven for 10-12 minutes at 400°F or Mark 6).

For mornay sauce
Melt the butter in a small pan, remove from heat and stir in the flour. Blend in half the milk, then stir in the rest. Stir this over moderate heat until boiling, then boil gently for 1-2 minutes. Remove from heat and gradually stir in grated cheese. Reheat but do not boil.

Oranges in caramel

8 large seedless oranges
(Navel are best)

For caramel
8 oz granulated sugar
$\frac{1}{4}$ pint cold water
$\frac{1}{4}$ pint warm water

8 cocktail sticks

Method

Put the sugar and cold water in a pan and
dissolve sugar over a very gentle heat.

Watchpoint Dissolve sugar slowly and boil
steadily to prevent it crystallising; keep
the heat under the pan very low as the
water should not boil until every grain of
sugar has dissolved. Do not stir. The sugar
can be moved from the bottom of the pan
by drawing a spoon carefully through it.

When all the sugar has dissolved, bring
to the boil and then cook steadily to a rich
brown caramel. Hold the pan over a bowl of
lukewarm water so that the base just
touches water (to prevent further cooking).
Cover the hand holding the saucepan with
a cloth (mixture may splash and scald) and
quickly pour in warm water; replace pan
on heat to dissolve caramel in the water,
then pour into a jug or a bowl and leave to
cool.

Pare a little rind from 1 orange, using a
potato peeler, cut into needle-like shreds,
cook for 1 minute in boiling water, then
drain and dry.

Cut the rind, pith and first membrane
from the oranges, leaving the flesh exposed.
This is best done with a serrated-edge knife
and, if you cut round with a sawing action,
you should not lose any juice.

Hold each orange at top and bottom in
your hand over a bowl and cut across in
slices. Hold these slices together with a
cocktail stick; arrange in a deep glass dish,
pour caramel on top, sprinkle over the
shredded orange rind and chill well.

4 oz butter
4 oz demerara sugar
4 oz golden syrup
4 oz plain flour
pinch of salt
1 teaspoon ground
  ginger
1 teaspoon lemon
  juice
2-3 drops of vanilla
  essence

For serving
$\frac{1}{4}$ pint double cream

This quantity makes about 20, and $\frac{1}{4}$ pint of double cream will fill 8-12 brandy snaps.

Method
Set the oven at 325°F or Mark 3. Put the butter, sugar and syrup into a saucepan and heat gently until the butter has melted and sugar dissolved. Leave to cool slightly. Sift flour with salt and ginger into mixture, stir well, adding lemon juice and vanilla essence.

Put teaspoons of mixture on a well-greased baking sheet at least 4 inches apart and cook in pre-set oven for 8 minutes. Leave biscuits for 2-3 minutes, then remove from the tin with a sharp knife, turn over and roll round the handle of a wooden spoon. Store in an airtight tin as soon as they are cold. Serve, filled with whipped cream.

Gratin of seafood

1¼ lb cod fillet, or
   4 frozen cod steaks
juice of ½ lemon
2 oz button mushrooms
4 oz prawns (shelled)
½ pint milk
slice of onion
6 peppercorns
blade of mace
1 oz butter
1 oz plain flour
salt and pepper
1 tablespoon Parmesan cheese
   (grated)

4 individual gratin dishes

Method

Set the oven at 350°F or Mark 4. If using fresh cod, discard the skin and cut fillets into fine strips. Grease 4 individual ovenproof gratin dishes (preferably with butter), put in fish and sprinkle with lemon juice. If using frozen cod, thaw, place in gratin dishes and sprinkle with lemon juice.

Wash mushrooms quickly in salted water, trim away stalks and then cut in fine slices. Sprinkle mushrooms and prawns on to the fish strips.

Put milk in a pan with the onion, peppercorns and mace, warm and remove from heat. Cover pan and leave to infuse until milk is well flavoured (at least 15 minutes). Strain the milk. Melt butter in a saucepan, remove pan from heat and blend in flour and flavoured milk. Season, stir over gentle heat until boiling, then simmer for 1 minute. Adjust the seasoning.

Spoon sauce over the fish, sprinkle with Parmesan cheese, bake for 20-25 minutes in preset oven until golden-brown.

Menu 4 Lamb

Starter : Eggs mimosa

Main course : Loin of Lamb Doria, Orange and redcurrant sauce, Anna potatoes

Dessert : Plum compote with rich almond cake

TIMETABLE

Day before
Make plum compote, cover and keep in refrigerator. Make almond cake and store in an airtight tin.
Put prawns to thaw in refrigerator.

Morning
Make orange and redcurrant sauce, set aside.
Peel and cut cucumber, blanch and refresh ; prepare onions, blanch and refresh. Put in pan or casserole with butter, season, leave ready for cooking. Peel potatoes, leave in bowl of cold water, do not slice.
Brown chine bone from lamb, and prepare stock for gravy.
Boil, but do not peel, eggs for eggs mimosa.

Assemble ingredients and dishes for final cooking from 6.00 for dinner around 8 pm.

Order of work

6.00　Prepare eggs mimosa, but do not coat with mayonnaise yet.
　　　Slice and butter brown bread and cover.

6.15　Dish up plum compote and almond cake.

Set oven at 400°F or Mark 6.
Put meat into oven.
Dry potatoes and butter pan. Slice potatoes and arrange in dish, cover with foil and a plate to weight them down.

6.50　Baste meat

7.00　Turn and baste meat again.
　　　Put potatoes over a steady but not fierce heat for 15 minutes.
　　　Baste meat, put potatoes into oven under meat.

7.30　Turn electric oven off or lower gas oven to Mark 4.
　　　Take out meat.
　　　Put meat on ovenproof plate or convenient dish and return to oven, either under or on same shelf as potatoes.
　　　Drain off fat from roasting tin, make gravy, strain and keep it hot.
　　　Coat eggs with mayonnaise.
　　　Cook cucumber and onions. Carve meat and arrange on dish with cucumber garnish.
　　　Turn out potatoes.

8.00　Serve first course.

Eggs mimosa

4 large eggs (hard-boiled)
4-6 oz shrimps, or prawns
   (shelled and coarsely chopped)
$\frac{1}{2}$ pint thick mayonnaise
   (see page 154)
watercress (to garnish)

Method
Cool eggs and peel. Split them in half lengthways, scoop out yolks and carefully push half of them through a bowl strainer into a basin. Add the shrimps or prawns. Mix and bind with 1-2 tablespoons mayonnaise.

Wash whites, dry and set on a serving dish. Fill with the prawn mixture. Thin the rest of the mayonnaise slightly with 1 tablespoon hot water and coat the eggs with this.

Hold strainer over eggs and push rest of the yolks through. Garnish dish with watercress.

Eggs mimosa is one of the best and simplest egg dishes for a first course. Garnish with watercress and serve with brown bread and butter

Loin of lamb Doria

2-2½ lb loin of lamb (chine, but
   reserve bone)
1 onion (quartered)
1 carrot (quartered)
1½ pints water
salt and pepper
bouquet garni
2-3 tablespoons dripping
1 large cucumber
2 bunches of spring onions, or
   12-18 pickling onions
¾ oz butter
1 dessertspoon flour
1 teaspoon parsley (chopped)

Method

Ask your butcher to chine the
loin of lamb.

Set oven at 400°F or Mark 6.

Place the chine bone from the
meat in the roasting tin without
any fat, and put into oven. Leave
to brown lightly in its own fat
while preparing the other ingredients (about 15 minutes).

Lift the bone into a saucepan,
add the onion and carrot and
pour over the cold water, season
and add bouquet garni. Bring
liquid slowly to the boil, skim
well and simmer for about 1
hour; then strain it.

Heat the dripping in the
roasting tin until smoking, put in
the meat and baste well. Roast
for 1-1¼ hours until tender. Baste
meat regularly and turn when
half cooked.

Peel the cucumber, split in
four lengthways and cut across
in 2-inch pieces. Trim the onions
and, if using spring onions,
leave on about 2 inches of the
green top. Blanch both vegetables in pan of boiling water
for 1 minute and drain well.

Melt the butter in a shallow
pan, add the onions and cucumber, season, cover and simmer for 5-8 minutes. Shake the
pan occasionally and as soon
as the cucumber is tender draw
pan aside and add the parsley.
Watchpoint If you are not ready
to serve the meal, let the cucumber and onion get cold and
reheat later; if cucumber is kept
hot or is overcooked, it gets very
watery.

When the meat is ready, take
up and set on a hot dish. Tilt the
roasting tin carefully and pour
off the dripping, leaving any
sediment behind. Dust the pan
with a very little flour (this
should only be enough to 'dry'
the tin), blend in over gentle
heat and cook until well coloured. Then pour on the stock
made from the chine bone. Stir
until boiling, then simmer until
well reduced. Taste gravy for
seasoning and serve in a gravy
boat.

Garnish the meat with the
cucumber mixture; serve with
orange and redcurrant sauce and
Anna potatoes (see page 40).

*The finished lamb Doria with gar-
nish of cucumber and spring onions*

Plum compote

1 lb red plums
1 wineglass red wine, or port
4 tablespoons redcurrant jelly (see page 156)
grated rind and juice of 1 orange

Method

Pour wine into a pan large enough to take the plums, boil until reduced to half the quantity. Add redcurrant jelly, stir gently until dissolved, then add the orange rind and juice.

Halve and stone the plums and put rounded side down (cut side uppermost) in the pan; let syrup boil up and over fruit, then poach gently until fruit is quite tender. Allow a full 10 minutes for this, even if the fruit is ripe.

Turn fruit into a bowl to cool; serve with a rich almond cake.

For rich almond cake
4 oz butter
5 oz caster sugar
3 eggs
3 oz ground almonds
1½ oz flour
2-3 drops of almond essence

Deep 7-inch diameter sandwich tin

Method

Grease and flour sandwich tin, cover base with disc of grease-proof paper; set the oven at 350°F or Mark 4.

Soften butter with a wooden spoon in a bowl, add the sugar a tablespoon at a time, and beat thoroughly until mixture is soft and light. Add the eggs, one at a time, adding one-third of the almonds with each egg. Beat well. Fold in the flour and almond essence with a metal spoon and turn cake mixture into the prepared tin.

Bake in pre-set oven for 45-50 minutes until cake is cooked. (Test by inserting a thin skewer; it should come out clean.) When cooked, the cake should also shrink very slightly from the sides of the tin.

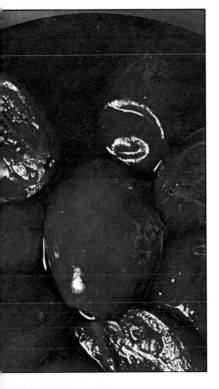

To turn out, have ready two wire cooling racks, put a clean folded tea towel or single thickness of absorbent paper on one of them. Loosen the sides of cake with a round-bladed knife, place the rack with the towel or paper on top of the cake (towel next to it) and turn over; remove the tin and disc of paper from the base.

Place second rack on top of cake base and carefully and quickly turn it over again. This prevents the rack marking top of cake. Dust top with caster sugar.

39

Orange and redcurrant sauce

juice and grated rind of 1 orange
4 tablespoons redcurrant jelly (see
 page 156)
1-2 teaspoons preserved mint
1 tablespoon white wine vinegar

Method
Grate the rind of the orange very finely, taking great care to remove the zest only and none of the white pith; mix with the juice in a bowl. Add this orange juice to the redcurrant jelly and stir gently until well mixed. If your jelly is very firm, warm it carefully in a saucepan before adding the orange rind and juice.

Add the mint and vinegar and serve in a small bowl or sauce boat.

Anna potatoes

1½-2 lb potatoes
salt and pepper
2-3 oz butter

*6-inch diameter thick frying pan
 with ovenproof handle, or cake tin*

*Using a mandoline slicer to cut
potatoes into very thin slices*

Method
Butter the frying pan or tin very generously. Slice the potatoes in thin rounds (a mandoline slicer is excellent for this) and arrange neatly in circles to cover the base of the pan. After two layers are in, season and add a few small pieces of butter. Continue to fill the pan, seasoning and buttering every other layer. Spread any remaining butter on a piece of foil and cover the pan securely.

Sit an ovenproof plate on top of the foil to give a little weight and prevent loss of steam during cooking. Set the pan on moderate heat for 15 minutes then put in the oven (below the meat) for about 30 minutes to complete the cooking. Turn out whole on to serving dish.

These two recipes are accompaniments to loin of lamb Doria (see page 36).

Menu 5 Lamb

Starter : Salmon mousse
Alternative : Herring pâté

Main course : Pot roast leg of lamb

Dessert : Danish raspberry shortcake

TIMETABLE

Day before
Make court bouillon, cook the salmon, and prepare béchamel sauce for mousse.
Make the aspic jelly.
Make jellied stock for lamb if none already made.
Make pastry and redcurrant glaze for raspberry short-cake.
Complete salmon mousse (coat top with aspic jelly when it is on the point of setting). If using frozen raspberries for shortcake, leave them overnight to thaw out in the refrigerator. (Make herring pâté.)

Morning
Bake the shortcrust pastry.
Open cans of vegetables and drain them ; thaw out petits pois and drain them.
Cover lamb with garlic and parsley butter.

Assemble ingredients and equipment for final cooking from 5.15 for dinner around 8 pm.

Order of work

5.15 Set oven at 375°F or Mark 5 ; put plates in warming drawer.
Arrange fruit on top to cover pastry case, glaze and decorate with cream, if wished.
Start cooking the lamb.
Make cucumber salad.

6.00 Add wine to lamb ; when it's reduced, put casserole in oven. Look at lamb after 30 minutes as you may need to reduce heat.

7.30 Strain gravy from lamb and add vegetables to casserole.
Turn oven to lowest setting.
Prepare sauce for lamb.
Dish up meat, garnish and serve remaining vegetables separately.

8.00 Serve first course.

Salmon mousse

$\frac{3}{4}$ lb salmon steak

For court bouillon
$\frac{3}{4}$ pint water
juice of $\frac{1}{4}$ lemon, or 1 wineglass
   white wine
$\frac{1}{2}$ teaspoon salt
3 peppercorns
bouquet garni

For béchamel sauce
$\frac{3}{4}$ cup of milk
$\frac{1}{2}$ bayleaf
1 blade of mace
6 peppercorns
1 slice of onion
3 oz butter
1 oz flour
salt
2 tablespoons double cream
   (lightly whipped)
1 tablespoon medium sherry
2 drops of carmine colouring
   (optional)

To finish
$\frac{1}{2}$ pint aspic jelly (cool but still
   liquid see page 150)
$\frac{1}{4}$ cucumber (thinly sliced)

*6-inch diameter top (No. 2 size)
soufflé dish*

This is a very rich mousse and you serve about 1 tablespoon as a portion. Serve with Melba toast.

Method
Place ingredients for court bouillon in a pan, bring to the boil, cover and simmer for 8-10 minutes. Strain. Put the salmon in a large pan, cover it with the hot court bouillon, bring this to the boil, then reduce the heat. Cover the pan and cook salmon very gently for 15 minutes; allow fish to cool in the liquid, then drain it on absorbent paper and remove all the skin and bone.

Watchpoint The court bouillon must just 'tremble' throughout the cooking time. If you want to cook the salmon in the oven, cover it with greaseproof paper and baste it frequently; allow 30 minutes at 325°F or Mark 4 (settings aren't comparable for this).

To prepare béchamel sauce; infuse the milk with seasonings, strain it when well flavoured and cool it slightly. Melt 1 oz butter in a pan, blend in the flour and milk. Add salt, stir sauce over gentle heat until boiling and cook for 2-3 minutes, then turn on to a plate to cool.

Cream the remaining butter until soft and lightly whip the cream. Work the salmon in a bowl with a wooden spoon or the end of a rolling pin, or pound

Pounding salmon for the mousse breaks down the fibres of the fish so that it will hold the béchamel sauce and butter without curdling

with a pestle in a mortar.

Watchpoint Pounding the salmon is important : this breaks down the fibres of the fish and it will then held the sauce and butter without them curdling.

Add the cold béchamel sauce and butter to the salmon and taste for seasoning. Fold in the cream and sherry. Add the carmine if the salmon is a very pale colour.

Turn mousse into soufflé dish, smooth the top with a palette knife and set in a cool place for about 10 minutes to firm. Pour over a thin layer of aspic jelly and when set arrange the cucumber on top, dipping each slice first in liquid aspic. When this garnish is set in position fill dish to the top with the remaining aspic.

Pot roast leg of lamb

3½-4 lb leg of lamb
2 oz butter
½ clove of garlic (crushed with
   ¼ teaspoon salt) - optional
1 tablespoon chopped parsley
1 wineglass white wine
1 wineglass jellied stock
salt
black pepper (ground from mill)

1 small can new potatoes
1 small can carrots
1 small can broad beans
1 small packet of frozen petits
   pois
1 teaspoon sugar
1 tablespoon flour
1 small carton (about 3 fl oz)
   single cream

Method

Ask your butcher to remove the shank bone from the leg of lamb. Use bone to make the jellied stock (see page 36). Cut away the fine skin and any fat that is covering the joint.

Soften the butter in a bowl with a wooden spoon, work in the crushed garlic and the parsley; spread this butter over the lamb and leave it for about 15 minutes. Then put the prepared joint in a large, heavy flame-proof casserole, cover and set over a gentle heat for about 30 minutes. Shake the pan occasionally during this period to prevent the lamb from sticking; at the end of this time the lamb should have changed colour (from pink to grey) but it should not be brown.

Set oven at 375°F or Mark 5. Now pour the wine into the casserole and leave it bubbling gently until it has reduced by about one-third, then pour on stock and season. Cover the pan and put in the pre-set oven for about 1-1½ hours.

Watchpoint Look at the joint after the first 30 minutes; if your casserole is of enamelled iron (as opposed to earthenware), you will probably need to lower the heat of the oven to 325°F or Mark 3. The meat should cook gently.

Strain the gravy from casserole but do not remove the meat. Drain the potatoes, carrots and broad beans and put in the casserole with the peas and the sugar, cover casserole and return to the oven. Turn the oven to its lowest setting while preparing the sauce.

To prepare sauce: skim fat from the cooking liquor, mix with the flour and return to the liquid. Tip this into a small pan and stir until boiling; then simmer for 2-3 minutes. Add the cream and reheat; taste the sauce for seasoning.

Dish up the meat, surround with vegetables (enough to make it look pretty but not to get in the way of the carver) and spoon over a little sauce. Pour the rest of the sauce over the vegetables, which should be served in a deep dish.

Danish raspberry shortcake

1 lb raspberries (frozen, or fresh in season)
3 tablespoons redcurrant glaze (see page 156)
1 small carton (about 3 fl oz) of double
   cream (whipped) - optional

For pastry
4 oz flour
3 oz butter
$1\frac{1}{4}$ oz icing sugar (sifted)
1 egg yolk
2-3 drops of vanilla essence

We have found that if you buy raspberries frozen **without** sugar, which are packed in a **rigid** container, and leave them to thaw overnight at refrigerated temperature, they will be quite dry and will look and taste like the freshly picked fruit. If you cannot find these, you should use a firmer fruit such as pineapple or apricots with an apricot glaze. Do not use canned raspberries as they are too soft to glaze.

Method

First prepare pastry: sift the flour on to a board or marble slab, make a well in the middle and put all the other ingredients in this. Work them to a smooth paste with the fingertips of one hand, drawing in the flour gradually; then chill pastry in refrigerator for 30 minutes.

Meanwhile set oven at 375°F or Mark 5. Roll or pat out pastry to a round, $\frac{1}{4}$ inch thick and 7-8 inches in diameter, slide it on to a baking sheet and bake blind in preset oven for about 15-20 minutes. The pastry should not brown but look like shortbread.

When pastry is cool, cover it with the raspberries and brush with redcurrant glaze. When quite cold, decorate shortcake with whipped cream or serve it separately.

Watchpoint If you choose canned fruit, it is wise to make double the quantity of glaze and brush the shortcake with a thin coating of this, then leave it to set before arranging drained fruit on top. This will prevent juices from the canned fruit on top soaking into the pastry. Glaze a second time on top of the fruit.

Dessert

Brush the redcurrant glaze thickly over the raspberries and leave it to set before decorating with cream

Whip the cream and use a forcing bag with a vegetable rose nozzle to pipe round an attractive border

Herring pâté

3 **buckling (smoked herrings)**
salt
pepper (ground from mill)
juice of ½ lemon
2 **tablespoons white wine**
½ **lb fresh cod, or haddock, fillet**
8 **tablespoons white breadcrumbs**
1 **egg yolk**
1 **oz butter (melted)**
1-2 **tablespoons double cream**
1 **bayleaf**

1-2 small terrines (oval ovenproof dishes with lids)

Method
Remove the skin and bones from the buckling and cut the flesh of two of them into finger-length pieces. Sprinkle with salt and pepper, pour over the lemon juice and wine and leave in this marinade for about 2 hours. Turn fish from time to time.

Meanwhile mince or pound the white fish with the remaining buckling and add the breadcrumbs, egg yolk, butter and cream. Stir in strained marinade and season to taste. Cover the bottom of the terrines with a layer of this mixture, then a layer of buckling pieces and repeat until all the ingredients are used, finishing with the white fish mixture. Put ½ bayleaf on top of each terrine, cover with foil, put on the lids and bake au bain marie in oven at 325°F or Mark 3 for about 45 minutes.

Remove lids and foil, leave pâté to cool, then cover with grease-proof paper and put a 1 lb weight on top of each one; leave overnight. Pour a little extra melted butter on the tops and leave to set. Serve with freshly made toast and pats of unsalted butter.

Menu 6 Pork

Starter : Cream of spinach soup

Main course : Roast pork périgourdine

Dessert : Rice cream with mandarins
Savoury : Devilled herring roes

TIMETABLE

Morning
Make rice cream and leave
to set, in a cool larder for pre-
ference. If keeping it in refrigerator, take out an hour
before dishing up.
Make soup, sieve and add milk
and seasoning ready for
reheating.
Make croûtons or hard-boiled
eggs to garnish soup.
Make demi-glace sauce for
pork. Bone out the pork ;
prepare it and set in a dish
ready for cooking.
Scrub potatoes, peel and cut
marrow.

Assemble ingredients and
equipment for final cooking
from 5.00 for dinner
around 8pm.

Order of work

5.00 Set oven and put in pork
to cook ; baste every 30
minutes.
Dish up rice cream and
decorate. (Cut bread, make
anchovy butter and scald
roes if serving savoury.)

7.10 Cook potatoes.
Put crackling into oven
to cook for 50-60 minutes.

7.30 Skin and slice potatoes,
cook shallots, add them to
potatoes and put in coolest
part of oven.
Cook marrow and leave in
covered pan to keep warm.

7.40 Turn oven to lowest
setting.

7.45 Put soup on to reheat
and add the cream.
(Fry the herring roes.)
Slice the pork, place on
a serving dish and spoon
over juices from the roasting dish. Heat demi-glace
sauce and keep warm.
Cover the meat with foil.
Dish up marrow.
Dish up and garnish soup.

8.00 Serve first course.
(Make toast and sauce for
devilled herring roes just
before serving them.)

49

Cream of spinach soup

$1\frac{1}{2}$ lb spinach
$1\frac{1}{4}$ oz butter
1 shallot (finely chopped)
1 oz flour
1 pint chicken, or vegetable, stock
  (see page 151)
salt and pepper
$\frac{1}{2}$ pint milk
little grated nutmeg
2-3 tablespoons double cream

For garnish
croûtons of fried bread (see page
  89), or lightly whipped cream and
  lemon slices, or hard-boiled egg

Method

Pick over the spinach, remove the stalks and wash thoroughly in several waters. Cook it for 3 minutes in boiling salted water to set the colour. Drain and then press spinach between two plates to remove as much water as possible.

Melt the butter, add the shallot and cook for 2-3 minutes until soft, but not coloured. Blend in the flour and continue cooking until the colour of straw. Tip on the stock, add the spinach, season and stir until boiling; cover and simmer for 20 minutes. Rub through a fine nylon sieve or purée in a blender. Return the soup to the saucepan and then add the milk to give a creamy consistency; taste for seasoning and add a small pinch of nutmeg.

If serving in a hot tureen, stir in the cream while soup is in the saucepan and reheat without boiling. Hand croûtons separately. If serving in soup cups and saucers, put a spoonful of lightly whipped cream and a slice of lemon in each cup after filling, or serve a quarter of hardboiled egg with each one.

Starter

Far left : removing stalks from spinach
Left : sieving the cooked spinach

Roast pork périgourdine

4 lb loin, or $\frac{1}{2}$ leg, of pork
salt
pepper (ground from mill)
1 clove of garlic
$\frac{1}{4}$-$\frac{1}{2}$ pint water
$\frac{1}{2}$ pint demi-glace sauce
  (to serve) — see method, page 13

Method

Set oven at 325°F or Mark 3. Remove the skin and bone from the loin or leg, flatten the meat and season very well with salt and pepper. Split the garlic into 5-6 thin shreds and place these along the meat. Roll the meat and tie securely, sprinkle again with salt and pepper and put into an ovenproof dish with $\frac{1}{4}$ pint water.
Note : if you want pork crackling, we suggest that when removing

the skin from the raw meat you cut away $\frac{1}{4}$ inch of fat with it. Cut this skin in strips and cook in a separate tin in the oven for 50-60 minutes, or until golden-brown and crisp. Serve lighly salted crackling as an accompaniment.

Cook the pork, allowing 40 minutes per lb, but not less than 2 hours for a smaller joint than given here. Baste it occasionally during the cooking, adding extra water when liquid reduces to a glaze. Meanwhile make the demi-glace sauce, if not done.

Take up the meat, remove the string and cut in thin slices, spoon over any juices left in the dish. Heat up the demi-glace sauce and hand separately.

Serve with maître d'hôtel potatoes and Hungarian marrow.

Main course

Maître d'hôtel potatoes

1½ lb even-size potatoes
1½ oz butter
1 shallot (chopped)
2 tablespoons chopped parsley
salt and pepper

Method

Scrub the potatoes and boil or steam them in their skins until tender but firm. Drain, dry and peel potatoes, slice and arrange in a hot ovenproof dish and keep warm.

Melt the butter in a small pan, add shallot, cover pan and set on low heat for 2-3 minutes. Then draw aside, add parsley and plenty of seasoning and pour over the potatoes. Slide them back into the oven for 2-3 minutes before serving.

Hungarian marrow

1 small young marrow
1-2 oz butter
1 dessertspoon paprika pepper
1 small onion (finely chopped)
2-3 tablespoons wine vinegar
about 6 dill, or caraway, seeds
1 teaspoon caster sugar
kneaded butter

Method

Peel marrow, cut into quarters, scoop out seeds and slice thinly. Melt 1-2 oz butter in a large pan. Put in the marrow and fry quickly for 4-5 minutes, shaking the pan well. Add the paprika. Take out the marrow and put in the onion, with more butter, if necessary.

Cover the pan for 1-2 minutes to cook the onion, then add the vinegar, dill (or caraway) seeds and the sugar. Thicken slightly with kneaded butter, replace the marrow, cover and simmer for 5 minutes, by which time it should be just tender.

Rice cream with mandarins

3 tablespoons thick grain rice
4-5 mandarins
1-1¼ pints milk
6 sugar lumps
scant ½ oz gelatine (see page 152)
little caster sugar (optional)
¼ pint double cream
1 egg white (optional)
extra double cream (to decorate) - optional

Fluted, or ring, mould (1¼ - 1½ pints capacity)

Method
Lightly oil the mould. Wash the rice, put it
in a pan with 1 pint of the milk and cook
over a slow heat until the grains are really
tender (about 30-35 minutes); if the
mixture gets too thick, add the remaining
milk. When cooked, the mixture should drop
easily from the spoon; turn it into a bowl
and cover with a plate.

Then rub the sugar lumps over the rind
of two of the mandarins until they are
soaked with the oil. Halve these mandarins
and squeeze them to extract the juice. Strain
this into a small pan, add the gelatine and
dissolve over a slow heat. While the rice is
still warm add the sugar lumps and stir until
dissolved. If additional sweetness is required, add some caster sugar. Then add
the gelatine mixture. Leave rice to get cold.

Meanwhile lightly whip the cream, whip-
ping the egg white in with it, if using this.
(The egg white lightens the mixture a little.)

When the rice is cold and beginning to
thicken, fold in the prepared cream. Turn
mixture into oiled mould and leave to set.

Pare a little of the rind from the remaining
mandarins, cut it into fine strips and blanch;
then drain and refresh. Separate the mandarins into sections and snip the edges of
these to remove any pips.

To serve; turn out the rice, sprinkle the
blanched rind over the top and arrange
mandarin sections round the edge, or fill
the centre with them if using a ring mould.
Decorate with extra cream, if wished.

Devilled herring roes

Savoury

½ lb soft herring roes
1 tablespoon seasoned flour
clarified butter (for frying)
4 slices of bread (for toast)
2 oz anchovy butter (see page 150)
1 oz butter
squeeze of lemon
point of cayenne pepper, or
    a dash of Tabasco sauce
paprika pepper

anchovy butter and cut in half;
arrange the herring roes on the
pieces of toast and place on a
hot dish.

Drop the 1 oz butter in the
pan, heat until nut-brown, then
add the lemon juice and cayenne
or Tabasco, and while this mixture is foaming pour it over the
roes. Dust with paprika and
serve very hot.

Method
Wash the herring roes, put them
in a colander and pour over a
jug of boiling water, drain well.
When cool roll them in seasoned
flour and fry in the clarified
butter until brown and crisp.
Wipe out the pan with absorbent
kitchen paper and keep on one
side.

Make the toast, trimming away
the crusts, spread with the

Devilled herring roes on anchovy toasts should be served very hot

Menu 7 Pork

Starter : Pineapple jelly salad

Main course : Pork tenderloin with prunes, Julienne of celery and potato

Dessert : Dacquoise

TIMETABLE

Day before
Make pineapple jelly salad and leave, covered, in cool larder. Make rounds for dacquoise and store unfilled ; soak apricots. Soak prunes overnight in tea.

Morning
Cook apricots and sieve ; make sugar syrup for sauce.
Drain prunes and stone.
Blanch almonds. Peel, wash and shred potatoes, leave in bowl of cold water until wanted for cooking. Wash and cut celery ; peel small onions and shallot and set aside.
Soak anchovies in a little milk to remove excess salt, drain, wrap around blanched almonds and stuff prunes for pork garnish. Cut and stuff pork fillets, tie neatly.
Cook onions for garnish and drain ; when cold, replace in pan with $\frac{1}{2}$ oz butter ready for reheating. Cook remaining prunes in wine, set aside to cool.
Assemble ingredients and equipment for final cooking from 5.30 for dinner around 8 pm.

Order of work

5.30 Whip cream, flavour with apricot purée and fill dacquoise ; decorate and dish up. Thin remaining purée with syrup.

6.00 Brown pork fillets, pour on stock, blend and bring to boil. Reduce heat and simmer for 40 minutes. Cook shallot and celery and leave in pan off heat.

6.30 Make dressing for pineapple jelly salad. Turn salad out of mould, fill centre with watercress. Cut brown bread and butter.

7.00 Set oven at 250°F or Mark $\frac{1}{4}$ and put serving dishes and plates to warm. Heat prunes in the wine.
Carve pork, set in hot serving dish and finish sauce. Spoon sauce over pork, cover and put in oven. Put prunes on top of cooked onions in pan and place over very low heat.

7.20 Drain potatoes, put in pan with celery mixture, cover tightly, cook over moderate heat, or in oven.
Put pans of onion and prune garnish into oven to keep hot.

7.55 Put onion and prune garnish on pork and dish up julienne of celery and potato.
Keep hot.

8.00 Serve first course.

57

Pineapple jelly salad

1 large can (approximately 24 fl oz)
  pineapple juice
juice of 2 large oranges (strained)
2 wineglasses dry white wine, or
  water
1 tablespoon white wine vinegar
1 oz gelatine (soaked in 5-6
  tablespoons cold water) — see right
6 tablespoons canned pineapple
  (diced)
1 bunch of watercress

For dressing
2 packets of Demi-Sel cheese,
  or 4 oz cream cheese
$\frac{1}{4}$ pint single cream
salt and pepper

Ring mould (2-2$\frac{1}{2}$ pints capacity)

Method

Combine the pineapple and strained orange juices with the wine (or water) and vinegar in a large pan.

Watchpoint Do not use the syrup from a can of pineapple pieces because this would be too sweet.

Make up this liquid to 1$\frac{1}{2}$ pints with more juice or water, if necessary.

Dissolve the soaked gelatine in a pan and when quite hot add to the liquid; pour about one-third into the wet mould and leave in a cold place until almost set.

Arrange diced pineapple in the mould and fill up with remaining cool, but still liquid, jelly. Cover and leave for 2-3 hours in refrigerator or overnight in a cool larder before turning out.

To prepare dressing; rub cheese through a wire strainer into a bowl and beat in the cream a little at a time. Season to taste, then pour the dressing into a small bowl or sauce boat for serving.

Turn out the jelly on to a flat serving plate and fill the centre with watercress

Watchpoint To turn out the jelly, dip the mould quickly in and out of a bowl containing hot water. Wipe the outside of the mould and then put the plate over the top and turn it upside down. Holding the plate and mould, give them a smart shake from side to side (not up and down, which would spoil the shape), then lift away the mould.

Serve with brown bread and butter and dressing separately.

Top : arranging diced pineapple over gelatine mixture (which is almost set) in the ring mould

Above : dipping pineapple jelly in hot water to loosen it from sides of ring mould before turning out

Gelatine. The best is obtained from simmering calves feet in water and is especially delicate in flavour. Most powdered gelatine is obtained from the bones or tissues of animals or fish by boiling. Always use a good quality gelatine and check the amount required with manufacturers' directions

Pork tenderloin with prunes

2 **pork tenderloin (fat-free) fillets of even-size, cut from underside of loin (about 2 lb)**
18 **large prunes (soaked in tea)**
6 **anchovy fillets (soaked in milk)**
6 **almonds (blanched)**
1½ **oz butter**
1 **dessertspoon flour**
½ **pint jellied stock**
salt and pepper
2 **wineglasses red wine**
12 **pickling onions**
1 **teaspoon arrowroot (if necessary)**

1 *Make a slit down the length of the pork fillet, open it out gently. Stuff prunes with anchovy and almond*
2 *Lay a few stuffed prunes down the centre of one of the fillets of pork*
3 *Place second fillet over first one*
4 *Tie fillets together with string*

Method
Soak prunes overnight in freshly-brewed tea; stone just before using. Soak anchovy fillets in milk for 30 minutes.

Make a slit down length of each pork fillet and open out gently. Stuff 6 prunes with an anchovy fillet wrapped round a blanched almond (see page 155) and lay on one fillet; cover this fillet by laying second opened-out fillet on top, and tie fillets together firmly with string.

Brown the tied fillets in the butter on all sides in a shallow pan, dust the flour into the pan and cook for 2-3 minutes, then tip on the stock. Blend liquid until smooth, bring to the boil and season. Cover the pan and simmer gently for about 40 minutes. Meanwhile cook the remaining prunes by simmering in wine till tender and most of the wine evaporated. Boil onions in salted water until tender, drain and keep hot.

Take up meat, carve in slices (removing string), arrange in a hot serving dish. Tip wine from prunes into sauce from pork fillets, bring to the boil and, if necessary, thicken with arrowroot slaked (mixed) with 1 tablespoon stock or water. Adjust seasoning, spoon sauce over meat; garnish with remaining prunes and onions mixed together. Serve with a julienne of celery and potato (see recipe on page 64).

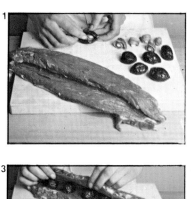

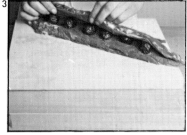

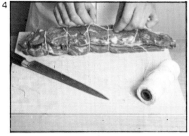

Dacquoise

3 oz almonds
4 egg whites
8 oz caster sugar
pinch of cream of tartar

For filling
4 oz dried apricots (soaked
    overnight in water)
strip of lemon rind
4 oz granulated sugar
$\frac{1}{4}$ pint water
juice of $\frac{1}{2}$ lemon
$\frac{1}{2}$ pint double cream
sugar (to taste)

For decoration
2 tablespoons icing sugar (sifted)
1 oz plain chocolate (grated)
extra double cream

*2 baking sheets lined with non-stick
    kitchen paper*

Method

Set the oven at 275°F or Mark 1.
Blanch the almonds, dry well and
pass them through a nut mill.
Watchpoint It is important for
this recipe that the almonds are
juicy and freshly ground, so if
you have only ready-blanched
almonds in your store cupboard,
pour boiling water over them
and leave them to soak for 10
minutes.

Whisk the egg whites until
stiff, add 1 tablespoon of the
caster sugar and the cream of
tartar and continue whisking for
1 minute. Fold in the remaining
caster sugar and the prepared
almonds.

Divide the mixture between
the baking sheets and spread

carefully into two rounds, 8
inches in diameter. Bake for
about 1 hour in the pre-set oven.
To test if the dacquoise is done,
lift the corner of the paper and
if it peels away from the bottom
the mixture is ready (if not,
continue baking until this
happens). Leave to cool.

Stew the apricots gently in
their soaking liquid with a strip
of lemon rind to flavour. When

tender, rub apricots through a fine sieve and leave them to cool.

Dissolve the granulated sugar in the water, add the lemon juice and boil for 3 minutes to make a sugar syrup. Whip the cream, sweeten to taste, and mix in a little of the apricot purée to flavour (about a quarter to a third); put into the dacquoise. Dust the top with icing sugar and decorate with rosettes of cream and grated chocolate (see photograph below). Dilute the remaining apricot purée with the sugar syrup and serve this sauce separately.

Finished dacquoise decorated with rosettes of cream and grated chocolate ; serve apricot sauce separately

Julienne of celery and potato

1 head of celery
3 even-size potatoes
1 oz butter
1 shallot (finely chopped)
salt
black pepper (ground from mill)
parsley (chopped) - to garnish

Serve as accompaniment to main course.

Method
Clean and trim celery stalks and peel potatoes. Cut them into julienne strips ($\frac{1}{8}$-inch thick by $1\frac{1}{2}$-2 inches long). Keep the potatoes in a bowl of cold water until wanted, to keep their colour and also remove some of the starch present.

Heat the butter in a sauté pan or flameproof casserole, add the celery and shallot, cover and shake over the heat for 4-5 minutes. The vegetables should not colour and this part of the cooking can be done well ahead.

Drain the potatoes and dry in a cloth; put them into the pan and season. Stir carefully to mix the celery and shallot into the potato, cover with greaseproof paper and a lid, and cook on top of the stove or in the oven until the potatoes are tender (8-10 minutes). Dust with chopped parsley and dish up.

Note : if this dish is prepared and cooked straight through and a shallow pan is used on top of the stove, the potatoes will take about 8-10 minutes. However, if the cooking time is broken and the potatoes are put into a cold celery mixture and then a moderate oven at 350°F or Mark 4, allow 15-20 minutes.

Menu 8 Gammon

Starter : Potage parabère

Main course : Baked gammon, Cumberland sauce and Leaf spinach

Dessert : Apple and hazelnut galette

TIMETABLE

Day before
Soak and cook gammon.
Make hazelnut pastry.
Cook apple filling.
Make Cumberland sauce.
Make soup but do not add
liaison. Cook garnish for soup.

Morning
Scrub potatoes thoroughly
and wash spinach.
Skin gammon, cover with
sugar topping and set in
roasting tin with cider
poured round.
Bake hazelnut pastry.
Cook spinach, drain, refresh
until quite cold and press
between two plates to remove
all water.

Assemble equipment for final
cooking from 6.30 for dinner
around 8 pm.

Order of work

6.30 Light oven. Assemble
dishes and plates and put
into warming drawer.
Put gammon into oven.
Baste gammon well and
put potatoes on to cook.
Chop and cook shallot
for potatoes. Baste gam-
mon again. If possible,
put skewers to heat in
gas flame.
Peel and slice cooked
potatoes and put in serving
dish ; pour over
cooked shallot and cover
with foil to keep
from drying out.

7.15 Add liaison and garnish
to soup. Set aside.

7.35 Turn oven to low setting ;
put in potatoes and take
out the gammon. Mark
gammon with hot skewers,
or caramelise under grill
if using electric stove.

7.45 Put soup on to heat.
Heat spinach in butter and
dish up.
Keep spinach and gammon
in warming drawer of stove.

8.00 Serve soup.

Potage parabère

4-5 medium-size onions (thinly sliced)
$1\frac{1}{2}$ oz butter
$1\frac{3}{4}$ pints veal, or chicken, stock
salt and pepper
kneaded butter (see method)
1 dessertspoon chopped parsley

For liaison
1 egg yolk
$2\frac{1}{2}$ fl oz single cream, or top of milk

For garnish

1 medium-size carrot
$\frac{1}{2}$ stick of celery
green part of leek

Method

Blanch the onions, drain thoroughly and
return to the pan with the butter. Cover
tightly and cook slowly until soft; do not
allow to colour. Draw pan aside, pour off
butter and reserve it. Pour on the stock,
season, bring to the boil and simmer until
onion is very tender (about 12-15 minutes).

Meanwhile make the garnish. Cut the
vegetables into thin strips and cook until
tender (6-7 minutes) in a little boiling
salted water.

When ready, rub onion mixture through a
fine sieve or work in a blender. Return onion
liquid to the rinsed-out pan and thicken a
little with kneaded butter, made with the
reserved melted butter and half as much
flour. The consistency of the soup should be
that of single cream.

Work the egg yolk with the cream (or
milk). Add to the soup as a liaison and
thicken slowly over the heat, without
allowing the soup to boil. Draw aside and
add the parsley. Drain garnish and add to
the soup. Serve hot.

Some of the ingredients needed for making potage parabère, a creamy onion soup garnished with thin strips of carrot, celery and leek

Baked gammon

4 lb gammon joint
1 onion
1 carrot
stick of celery
large bouquet garni
6 peppercorns
4 tablespoons soft brown, or demerara, sugar
grated rind and juice of 1 orange
large pinch of ground mace
½ pint cider

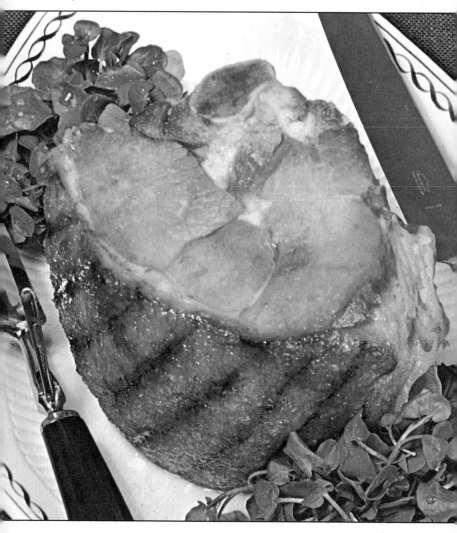

Method

Choose a prime lean cut, such as a corner gammon or a piece of middle gammon. Soak the joint for 4 hours in enough cold water to cover. (If very small, say about $1\frac{1}{2}$ lb, soak for 1 hour only.) Throw away water and cover joint again with fresh cold water. Bring slowly to the boil and skim well. Add vegetables and seasoning, cover, simmer very gently for $1-1\frac{1}{2}$ hours (1-2 lb joints), or 30 minutes per lb for joints over 3 lb.

When the gammon is cooked, strip off the skin. This is easily done by carefully lifting the corner with a knife and then pulling off with the fingers. If straight from the pan and very hot, hold the skin with kitchen paper or a cloth. Set joint in a baking tin.

Mix sugar, orange juice, rind and spice together and spread over skinned surface of the gammon. Pour the cider round. Bake in the oven at 350°-375°F or Mark 4 until golden-brown (20-30 minutes).

Score the top in the following way; if using an electric stove, caramelise the sugar crust by putting under a hot grill for 5-7 minutes until crisp and brown; if using a gas stove, heat two metal skewers in the flame until red hot. Take each skewer in turn and hold lightly on the sugar crust to burn in decorative lines.

Place gammon on a hot serving dish and keep in the warming drawer of the stove for 15 minutes before serving. This waiting time makes the gammon much easier to carve. Serve maître d'hôtel potatoes, see page 53, Cumberland sauce and leaf spinach.

Cumberland sauce

1 orange and its juice
4 tablespoons redcurrant jelly
  (see page 156)
juice of $\frac{1}{2}$ lemon
1 glass port wine

Method

Remove rind from a quarter of the orange with a potato peeler. Cut into needlelike shreds and cook in boiling water until tender, then drain and rinse well. Heat the redcurrant jelly until dissolved, then stir in the lemon juice, wine and strained juice of the orange. When cold, add the orange rind and serve.

Leaf spinach

2-3 lb spinach
$\frac{3}{4}$ oz butter

Method

Wash the spinach thoroughly, remove stalks and any thick centre ribs. Cook in plenty of boiling salted water for 5-8 minutes, then drain well in a colander. Press between two plates to get rid of as much water as possible.

Melt butter in a saucepan, allow to colour slightly, then add the spinach and toss until dry. Serve.

69

Apple and hazelnut galette

3 oz hazelnuts (shelled)
3 oz butter
2 rounded tablespoons caster
  sugar
4½ oz plain flour
pinch of salt

For filling
1 lb dessert apples (pippin variety)
1 tablespoon smooth apricot jam
grated rind of 1 lemon
1 tablespoon orange peel (finely
  chopped)
2 tablespoons sultanas
2 tablespoons currants
icing sugar (for dusting)
whipped cream (optional)

Method

Brown the shelled nuts in the oven at 350°F or Mark 4 until husks can be rubbed off (about 7-8 minutes when nuts should be a deep golden-brown). Reserve a few whole nuts for decoration and pass remainder through a small cheese grater or mincer, or work until fine in a blender.

Soften the butter, add sugar and beat together until light and fluffy. Sift the flour with a pinch of salt and stir into the mixture with the prepared nuts. Chill for at least 30 minutes.

Meanwhile prepare filling. Peel, core and slice the apples. Put them in a pan with apricot jam and grated lemon rind. Cook over slow heat until soft, then add orange peel, sultanas and currants; simmer for another 5 minutes.

Divide the pastry mixture in two and place each piece on a lightly-floured baking sheet. Roll or pat into very thin rounds 9 inches in diameter. Bake for about 10 minutes in the oven at 375°F or Mark 5.

Watchpoint Do not let pastry brown or it will taste scorched. While still warm and on the baking sheet, trim edges and cut one round into eight portions, then slide carefully on to a wire rack to cool.

Cover the whole round of pastry with apple mixture, spread evenly and place the cut portions on top. Dust with icing sugar. Serve with whipped cream, or pipe rosettes of cream on each portion and decorate with whole hazelnuts.

Rosettes of whipped cream piped on to each portion of the apple and hazelnut galette make an elegant decoration. Finish off with a hazelnut in the centre of each rosette

Menu 9 Capon

Starter : Vegetable bortsch

Main course : Capon à la crème

Dessert : Strawberry water ice, Fours aux amandes
With coffee : Chocolate truffles

TIMETABLE

Day before
Prepare and make vegetable
bortsch but do not add liaison.
Make syrup for strawberry
water ice, and fours aux
amandes. Make chocolate
truffles.

Morning
Prepare potatoes. (Prepare
green vegetables, if serving.)
Make and complete water
ice if a deep-freeze is
available for storing it ; if
not, leave churning until later.
If making it in refrigerator,
the ice can be completed and
left in ice-making compartment
of refrigerator.

Assemble equipment and
ingredients for final cooking
from 5.45 for dinner
around 8 pm.

Order of work

5.45 Start cooking capon.
Churn ice and pack down,
if this hasn't been done.

7.15 Cook potatoes. (Cook
chosen green vegetable.)
Grill bacon.
Take up capon, make
sauce and dish up. Cream
potatoes. Keep both warm.

7.50 Heat soup, adding liaison.

8.00 Serve first course.
Dish up water ice after
main course has been
eaten.

Vegetable bortsch

beetroot
onions
carrots
celery
parsnip
salt and pepper
stock (preferably ham), or water
cabbage (coarsely shredded)
garlic (chopped, or crushed) — to
   taste
tomatoes
sugar
little tomato purée
fresh parsley (chopped)

For liaison
little flour (optional)
soured cream

*5-inch diameter pudding basin
   (sufficient for 3 pints liquid), or
   small mixing bowl*

Quantities of vegetables should be used in the following proportions: half beetroot and of remaining half, one-third onion, one-third carrot and the last third equally divided between celery and parsnip.

Method
Cut beetroot, onions, carrots, celery and parsnip into matchsticks and pack into the basin or bowl to fill it.

Lightly season stock or water and bring to the boil. Turn the bowl of vegetables into the pan, cover and simmer for about 20-30 minutes. Coarsely shred enough cabbage to fill the bowl, add this with the garlic to taste. Continue to simmer gently, uncovered, for a further 20 minutes.

Skin sufficient tomatoes to half-fill the bowl, squeeze to remove seeds, then chop flesh very coarsely. Add to soup, season well with salt and sugar and add a little tomato purée to sharpen the flavour. Simmer for a further 10 minutes, then add a handful of chopped parsley.

The soup can be thickened lightly with a little flour mixed with a small quantity of soured cream. Otherwise serve a bowl of soured cream separately.

Watchpoint Bortsch should be slightly piquant in flavour and not sweet. Add salt and sugar until this is reached. The soup should be a thick broth of vegetables but not too solid. Dilute if necessary with additional stock.

This bortsch is improved if made the previous day.

Starter

A colourful show of vegetables for making bortsch, a soup that's slightly piquant in taste

Capon à la crème

1 capon (weighing 5-6 lb)
2 oz unsalted butter
¾ lb Spanish onions (sliced and blanched)
2½ fl oz brandy
about ¼ pint chicken stock (see page 151)
½ pint creamy béchamel sauce (see page 150)
7½ fl oz double cream

For garnish
¾ lb No. 4 cut back bacon rashers (smoked or
unsmoked)

Method

Melt the butter in a large pan, put in the
capon, cover the pan and set on low heat
so that the bird becomes white and does not
colour. This is known as 'whitening in
butter' and will take about 10-12 minutes.
Turn the bird occasionally but on no account
allow it to brown. Then take it out, put in
the onion, cover again and cook for 4-5
minutes so that the onion absorbs the
remaining butter. Replace the bird, add
brandy and a little of the stock. Cover and
cook slowly on top of cooker, or in the oven
at 350°F or Mark 4, until the capon is tender
(about 1-1½ hours).
Watchpoint If cooking bird on top of
cooker, add extra stock if pan gets dry.

Meanwhile prepare the bacon garnish:
remove the rust and rind from the rashers,
cut each in half and grill until crisp.

Take up the capon, dish up and keep warm.
Work the contents of the pan in a blender,
first adding the béchamel sauce. (A Mouli
sieve may be used, but a blender gives a
better result.) Turn the sauce into a saucepan
and reheat. Boil the cream until thick, reducing it to about ¼ pint, and add to the
sauce. Pour enough sauce over the capon
to coat nicely and serve the rest separately.
Pile the bacon garnish at one end of the dish.
Serve with purée potato.

Although a green vegetable of your choice
may be served with the capon, to appreciate
the delicate flavour of this dish it is best
eaten with just the purée potatoes and
bacon garnish. You can, of course, serve a
green vegetable as a separate course.

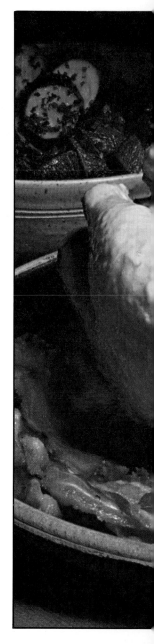

Capon à la crème : the finished dish

Strawberry water ice

1 lb strawberries
8 oz lump sugar
1 pint water
juice of $\frac{1}{2}$ lemon
grated rind and juice of 1 small orange
1 rounded dessertspoon whipped egg white
$\frac{1}{4}$ oz gelatine (for refrigerator method)

If fresh strawberries are not available, it is better to use those frozen without sugar. The ice can be made in an ice-cream churn or in a refrigerator; both methods are given.

Method

Put the sugar in a pan with the water, bring to the boil and boil steadily for 10-12 minutes (220°F on a sugar thermometer). Strain well, pour into a jug and add the lemon juice. Set aside to cool.

Meanwhile hull the strawberries and crush well with a fork. Add the grated rind and strained juice of the orange and turn mixture into a covered bowl; leave in the freezing compartment of refrigerator for about 30 minutes. Then add the cooled syrup. Turn into prepared ice-cream churn (see page 153) and churn to a slush. Then add the whipped egg white and continue to churn until firm. Remove dasher and pack down; leave until wanted.

Watchpoint If the strawberry water ice is left in the churn for longer than 1 hour, the melted ice will have to be drained off and the bucket replenished with fresh ice.

Note : if freezing the ice in a refrigerator, dissolve the $\frac{1}{4}$ ounce of gelatine in a small quantity of the sugar syrup after straining it. Add to the jug with the lemon juice. Chill before adding to strawberry mixture. Turn the refrigerator to the maximum freezing temperature, freeze to a slush, then beat in the required amount of egg white. Return to the ice compartment, freeze until just firm, then beat again; cover with foil and return to the ice compartment. At this stage the refrigerator can be turned back to normal and the ice left until required.

Serve in a well-chilled glass bowl, or coupe glasses, with fours aux amandes.

Fours aux amandes

4 oz ground almonds
3 oz caster sugar
2 egg whites
almond, or vanilla, essence
split almonds, glacé cherries and
    angelica (to decorate)
1 tablespoon caster sugar
    (dissolved in 2 tablespoons
    milk)

*Rice paper, or non-stick (siliconised)
kitchen paper; forcing bag and
coarse vegetable rose pipe*

Method
Set oven at 350°F or Mark 4.

Mix the almonds and sugar together and pass them through a wire sieve. Whisk egg whites until stiff and fold in the almonds and sugar with the flavouring essence.

Place the non-stick paper, or rice paper (smooth side down), on a dry baking sheet. Fill the forcing bag with the almond mixture. Pipe this on to the paper, making various shapes. Decorate each one with a split almond, or glacé cherry and angelica. Bake in pre-set oven for about 15 minutes.

As soon as cakes are cooked, brush tops with sugar and milk solution. When cold, break off surplus rice paper (if used).

Chocolate truffles

To serve with coffee

12 oz best dessert chocolate
about 4 fl oz strong black coffee
4 oz unsalted butter
4 oz ground praline powder
  (see page 155)
1 dessertspoon brandy, or rum
3 tablespoons double cream

To finish
2-3 oz dessert chocolate
2-3 tablespoons cocoa

Offer these to guest when serving the coffee. This quantity makes about 1 lb of truffles.

Method

Break up the 12 oz chocolate and put the pieces into a pan with the coffee. Set the pan on low heat and stir until the chocolate is melted, when it should be a thick cream; do not let it become too hot. Then draw pan aside, cool the mixture a little and add the butter a small piece at a time. Stir in the praline powder and brandy (or rum), then the cream.

Watchpoint The mixture must not be over-stirred while the cream is being added or it will not be stiff enough for shaping into balls.

Put the chocolate mixture out, a teaspoon at a time, on a sheet of greaseproof paper; shape into balls and leave to set.

To finish the truffles, melt the remaining dessert chocolate on a plate over a pan of warm water. Sprinkle the cocoa over a sheet of greaseproof paper.

Put a teaspoon of the melted chocolate in the palm of one hand, then roll a truffle first in this, then in the cocoa, and lift it on to a clean sheet of greaseproof paper. Continue in this way until all the truffles are coated; make sure, however, that you have just enough cocoa to coat them evenly. When the chocolate is set, it will give a crisp coating to the truffles.

Menu 10 Chicken

Starter : Délices of sole Parmesan

Main course : Spring chicken bonne femme

Savoury : Tomato and Gruyère toasts
Dessert : Orange soufflé nantaise

TIMETABLE

Morning
Cook belly pork and blanch
onions for chicken bonne
femme.
Make chicken stock and
scrape potatoes.
Season and truss poussins.
Make breadcrumbs and mix
with cheese for délices of
sole Parmesan.
Clarify butter for frying.
(Cut bread for savoury toasts ;
skin and slice tomatoes.)
Make the soufflé.

Assemble equipment and
ingredients for final cooking
from 6.00 for dinner
around 8 pm.

Order of work

6.00 Decorate soufflé and set
aside in a cool place.

6.30 Set the oven ; start
browning poussins and
potatoes.

6.45 Put poussins into oven
(unless cooking on top of
the stove).
Coat fish with egg and
crumb mixture.
Blanch onions.

7.15 Take up chicken and
potatoes ; keep warm in a
deep dish.
Turn oven to lowest set-
ting. Brown onions and
pork, then finish sauce
for poussins.
(Soak bread for savoury
toasts.)

7.40 Put French beans to cook.
Fry the fish and keep warm.
(Fry bread for savoury
toasts.)
Fry bananas and garnish
fish ; keep hot.
Drain beans and toss in
butter.
(Arrange cheese and
tomato on toasts and grill.)

8.00 Serve first course.

79

Délices of sole Parmesan

1½-2 lb lemon, or Dover, sole (filleted)
1 tablespoon seasoned flour
1 egg (beaten)
4 tablespoons fresh breadcrumbs (see page 150)
2 tablespoons Parmesan cheese (grated)
3 oz butter (clarified)
2 small bananas
½ oz butter
juice of ¼ lemon
8 almonds (blanched and shredded) - see page 155

Method

Cut the fillets of fish into thick finger-like strips and dry them well. Roll them in the seasoned flour, brush with egg and coat with the breadcrumbs and cheese mixed together, pressing them on to the fish with a palette knife. Then fry fillets in the clarified butter until crisp and golden-brown. Pile them into a hot serving dish (without draining) and keep warm.

Wipe out the frying pan with absorbent paper. Cut the bananas in thick slanting slices, drop the ½ oz butter in the pan and, when foaming, add the bananas and fry quickly until brown. Pour over the lemon juice and add the almonds. Arrange the bananas and almonds around the fish and serve very hot.

The banana slices which accompany the sole are fried quickly in foaming butter until brown

Délices of sole Parmesan : the finished dish ready to serve

Spring chicken bonne femme

4 poussins
4-6 oz belly pork
salt and pepper
2 oz butter
16 small new potatoes (scraped)
$7\frac{1}{2}$ fl oz chicken stock (see page 151)
bouquet garni
12 pickling onions, or shallots
1 dessertspoon arrowroot
2 tablespoons single cream, or top
  of the milk
1 tablespoon chopped parsley

Method
Put the pork in pan, cover with water and simmer for 45 minutes, then remove the skin and any small bones and cut into lardons.

Meanwhile season the inside of the poussins and truss them firmly. Melt $1\frac{1}{2}$ oz of the butter in a large stewpan, put in the poussins and potatoes and brown them slowly on all sides. Moisten with 5 tablespoons of stock, tuck in the bouquet garni, cover the pan tightly and cook gently on top of the stove for 20-30 minutes or in the oven at 350°F or Mark 4 for 30-35 minutes.

Blanch the onions in a pan of cold water brought to boiling point for 5 minutes, then drain them.

Take up the poussins, remove the trussing strings and keep the birds warm in a deep dish; lift the potatoes out of the pan with a draining spoon and keep warm with the chicken. Remove the bouquet garni. Drop the remaining $\frac{1}{2}$ oz butter into the pan and add the pork and onions. Cover and shake the pan occasionally until they are evenly browned and tender. Tip on the remaining stock, bring to the boil and thicken with the arrowroot mixed with the cream; add the chopped parsley and reboil. Either spoon sauce over the poussins and potatoes and serve or return the poussins and potatoes to the pan. Serve with French beans.

The poussins may be brought to the table with the sauce spooned over them; the whole dish is garnished with chopped parsley

Right : the cooked poussins in the pan with the pork and onions before being coated with sauce

Tomato and Gruyère toasts

1 egg (lightly beaten)
¼ pint milk
salt and pepper
3 slices of white bread
2 oz butter
1 teaspoon French mustard
   (preferably Dijon mustard)
3 oz Gruyère cheese (thinly sliced)
3 tomatoes
salt and pepper
1 sprig of rosemary

Method

Mix together the egg, milk, salt and pepper. Remove the crusts from the bread, cut each slice into three and soak in the egg and milk.

Meanwhile heat the butter in a frying pan, then fry the bread slowly so that a crust is formed at the bottom before the bread is turned and browned on the other side. Spread the fried bread very thinly with a good French mustard. Put in a warm shallow casserole ready for grilling and place the slices of Gruyère cheese on top.

Scald and skin the tomatoes

The pieces of bread (previously soaked in egg and milk) are fried in butter until crusly and golden-brown

Season the toasts before grilling, spike with rosemary and put a knob of butter on each tomato slice

(see page 156), cut the core from the top, squeeze gently to remove some of the seeds, then cut them in thick slices and arrange on top of the cheese. Season lightly and dust with sugar; spike the slices with a few leaves of rosemary. Put a tiny knob of butter on each tomato slice and grill until the cheese bubbles and begins to brown. Serve hot.

The tomato and Gruyère toasts, garnished with rosemary, ready to serve

Orange soufflé nantaise Dessert

4 tablespoons crushed
  macaroons (see page 154)
little Grand Marnier liqueur
3 large eggs (separated)
6 oz caster sugar
grated rind of 1 lemon
grated rind and strained juice of
  3 small oranges
$\frac{1}{2}$ pint double cream
$\frac{1}{2}$ oz gelatine (see page 152)
juice of $\frac{1}{2}$ lemon (made up to
  $2\frac{1}{2}$ fl oz with water)

For decoration
1 small carton (3 fl oz) double
  cream (whipped and sweetened)
2 tablespoons macaroon crumbs

6-inch diameter top (No. 2 size)
soufflé dish

Method

Tie a band of double grease-proof paper round the outside of the soufflé dish, standing up an inch or so above the dish to support the gelatine mixture until it has set. Soak the macaroons in the liqueur.

Place the egg yolks, sugar, lemon and orange rinds and strained orange juice together in a basin over hot water and whisk over gentle heat until the mixture is thick and mousse-like. Remove from the heat and continue whisking for 5 minutes or until the bowl is cool.

Lightly whip cream and fold it into the mixture. Dissolve the gelatine in the lemon juice and water and stir this liquid into the mixture. Whisk the egg whites until stiff but not dry, set bowl of soufflé mixture on ice and fold in egg whites. As the mixture begins to thicken, turn it into the soufflé dish, layering it with crushed macaroons; put in a cool place to set.

When firm run a hot palette knife between the two layers of greaseproof paper and peel paper off. Press remaining macaroon crumbs gently round the sides and decorate the top of the soufflé with rosettes of whipped, sweetened cream or as shown.

Menu 11 Chicken

Starter : Potage bonne femme

Main course : Coq au vin

Dessert : Cold lemon soufflé
Savoury : Roquefort tartlets

TIMETABLE

Day before
Prepare soup but do not
add liaison.
Cook coq au vin but do not
thicken the sauce ; turn into
a cold bowl or casserole
ready for reheating. Keep in
a cool place.
(Make pastry if preparing
savoury tartlets, and prepare
filling.)

Morning
Make soufflé but do not
decorate ; put in the
refrigerator.
(Line pastry into the tartlet
tins, fill and leave ready for
baking.)
Cut croûtes for chicken and
croûtons for soup and fry.
Peel potatoes and chop
parsley.

Assemble ingredients for
final cooking from 6.30 for
dinner around 8 pm.

Order of work
6.30 Remove paper from soufflé
and decorate.
Set oven at 375°F or
Mark 5 and arrange oven
shelves : one low for chicken
(one high for cheese
tartlets).
Put chicken to heat.
Warm croûtes and croûtons.

7.00 Put potatoes to cook.
(Put tartlets to bake.)

7.30 Turn oven to lowest
setting and leave chicken
(and tartlets) to keep
warm. Put plates to warm.

Mash potatoes to a purée
with seasoning and milk ;
cover with a 'lid' of hot
milk to prevent skin
forming.
Heat soup, add liaison,
then reheat.
Thicken sauce for chicken
and add garnishes. Stir in
milk just before serving
potatoes.

8.00 Serve first course.

Potage bonne femme

6 leeks
4 small potatoes
$2\frac{1}{2}$ oz butter
salt
pepper (ground from mill)
$\frac{3}{4}$ pint milk
$\frac{3}{4}$ pint water
2-3 slices stale bread (for croûtons)
fat (for frying croûtons)
2 egg yolks
$\frac{1}{4}$ pint single cream
1 teaspoon parsley (chopped)

Method

Wash and trim leeks very carefully as they can be gritty. Make a deep cross-cut through the leaves and wash under a fast-running tap. Slice the white parts only of 5 leeks, keeping the other aside for garnish. Peel and slice potatoes.

Melt the butter in a large pan, add the vegetables and seasoning and stir over a gentle heat until almost soft. When vegetables are well impregnated with the butter and have started to cook, cover them with a buttered paper and lid (this is known as sweating); there is no need to stir them all the time. Cook for at least 10 minutes.

Remove buttered paper, then pour on the milk and water and stir until boiling. Draw pan half off heat and half cover the pan with a lid; leave to simmer for 15 minutes.

Pass soup through a Mouli sieve or mix to a purée in an electric blender.

Cut the reserved leek into fine shreds with a knife, put into cold water and boil for 2 minutes. Drain and dry.

Make the croûtons. Drain them well and keep hot.

Return soup to clean pan and reheat. Work the egg yolks with cream in a bowl and add about 3-4 tablespoons of hot soup to this liaison. Pour this back into pan in a thin, steady stream and stir over a gentle heat until the soup thickens.

Watchpoint Do not let soup boil or the eggs will curdle. If this should happen, whisking will help the appearance.

Garnish soup with a little shredded leek and chopped parsley; serve the fried croûtons separately.

To make croûtons :
Take 4 or 5 slices of stale white bread and cut into tiny cubes. Fry these in fat (you can use either shallow or deep fat for frying croûtons) until they are golden brown. Remove from pan and drain thoroughly on absorbent paper. Salt lightly before serving.

Potage bonne femme — a leek and potato soup, served with croûtons

Coq au vin

$3\frac{1}{2}$-4 lb roasting chicken
4 oz gammon rashers
4 oz button onions
2 oz butter
$\frac{1}{4}$ bottle of Burgundy (7 fl oz)
2 cloves of garlic (crushed with
    $\frac{1}{2}$ teaspoon salt)
bouquet garni
$\frac{1}{2}$-$\frac{3}{4}$ pint chicken stock (see page 151)
salt and pepper
kneaded butter (made by working to
    a paste 2 parts butter to 1 part
    flour)

For garnish
1 French roll (for croûtes) —
    sliced
butter, or salad oil (for frying)
chopped parsley

Jointing the chicken after it has been browned in butter

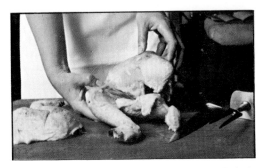

If good wine has been used for this dish it needs no accompanying vegetable except creamed potatoes.

Method

First truss the chicken or tie neatly. This is important even though the bird is jointed immediately after browning as it stays compact, making it easy to turn in casserole during browning.

Remove rind and rust from the bacon, cut into lardons, ($\frac{1}{4}$-inch thick strips, $1\frac{1}{2}$ inches long). Blanch these and onions by putting into a pan of cold water bringing to the boil and draining well.

Brown chicken slowly in butter, then remove from casserole. Add onions and lardons; while these are browning, joint chicken. Replace joints in casserole pan and 'flame' by pouring on wine and setting it alight. Add the crushed garlic, bouquet garni, stock and seasoning. Cover casserole and cook slowly for about 1 hour, either on top of stove, or in pre-set oven at 325°F or Mark 3.

To make croûtes : fry slices of bread on both sides in butter or oil until golden-brown.

Test to see if chicken is tender by piercing flesh of the thigh with a fine-pointed cooking knife. If clear liquid runs out, it is ready, if pink continue cooking. When ready remove chicken, bouquet garni and taste sauce for seasoning. Thicken slightly with kneaded butter, then dish up chicken in casserole with sauce. Surround with croûtes and sprinkle with chopped parsley. Serve with creamed potatoes.

91

Cold lemon soufflé

3 large, or 4 medium-size eggs (separated)
8 oz caster sugar
rind and juice of $2\frac{1}{2}$ lemons
$\frac{1}{2}$ oz gelatine (soaked in 5 tablespoons cold
    water) — see page 152
$\frac{1}{2}$ pint double cream
pistachio nuts, or browned almonds (finely
    chopped) — see page 155
extra double cream (whipped) — for decoration

6-inch diameter top (No. 2 size) soufflé dish

Method

Prepare the soufflé dish by tying a band of greaseproof paper round the outside (see page 86).

Put the egg yolks, sugar, finely grated lemon rind and juice in a basin over a pan of hot water and whisk until the sugar has dissolved and the mixture has thickened a little. Remove the basin from the pan and continue whisking until the bowl is cool. If using an electric beater on high speed, no heat is necessary.

Dissolve the gelatine in a pan over gentle heat. Whip the cream until it just begins to thicken and the whisk leaves a trail, then fold it into the soufflé mixture. Add the dissolved gelatine. Whisk the egg whites until stiff but not dry.

Watchpoint For a perfect soufflé the egg whites must be whisked by hand with a light wire whisk. A rotary beater makes them too solid so that by the time they are mixed into the soufflé they have lost a lot of bulk.

Stand the soufflé mixture in a bowl of cold water containing a few ice cubes. Cut and fold in the egg whites very carefully with a metal spoon. Stir the mixture until it begins to thicken, then pour at once into the prepared soufflé dish. Put in a cool place to set.

For serving, remove the paper and decorate the top with whipped cream and nuts.

Roquefort tartlets

For rich shortcrust pastry (see method , page 156)
6 oz plain flour
pinch of salt
4 oz butter
1 egg yolk
1-2 tablespoons cold water

For filling
¼ pint double cream
¼ pint béchamel sauce (made with ½ oz butter, 1 tablespoon flour, ¼ pint flavoured milk) — see page 150
4 oz Roquefort cheese (grated)
3 egg yolks

9 tartlet tins, or bun pan

Method

Prepare the pastry and set aside to chill. Set oven at 375°F or Mark 5.

Boil the cream until reduced by one-third, stir in the béchamel sauce and, while still warm, beat in the cheese and then egg yolks. Leave to cool.

Roll out the pastry, cut into rounds and line the tins. Cut a lid for each one from remaining pastry. Spoon the filling into the pastry cases — they should be three-quarters full — and sit a lid on top of each one. Bake for about 20 minutes in pre-set oven until golden-brown. Serve hot.

Serve Roquefort tartlets as a savoury alternative to the dessert

Menu 12 Duck

Starter : Fresh haddock mousse
Alternative : Potage madrilène

Main course : Roast duck Hymettus, Haricots verts béarnais

Dessert : Savarin Chantilly

TIMETABLE

Day before
Make haddock mousse and
mayonnaise, cover and keep
in a cool place. (Make chicken
stock). Make stuffing for
duck, store in basin. (Make
stock from giblets and keep
in a cool place).

Morning
(Skim chicken stock, make
soup and strain. Return to
clean, cold saucepan, cover
and leave ready for reheating.)
Stuff duck, truss and set in
tin ready for roasting.
Cook frozen beans and
refresh, leave in colander.
Chop and cook onions and
leave in the sauté pan ready
for evening. Cut bacon for
cooking. Prepare potatoes.
Make and bake savarin, soak
with prepared syrup.

Assemble the serving dishes
and equipment for final
cooking from 5.45 for dinner
around 8 pm.

Order of work

5.45 Set oven. Dish up savarin
and pour over kirsch or
rum if being used.

6.00 Put duck in oven.

6.30 Baste and turn duck.
Turn out fish mousse,
mask with mayonnaise and
garnish.

7.00 Put potatoes to cook.
Baste and turn duck.

7.25 Drain potatoes, keep warm
in pan with folded teacloth
or napkin on top to absorb
steam.
Heat onion and cook bacon
for beans.
Take up duck. Make gravy.
Put soup to heat.
Toss beans with onion and
bacon till hot, dish up.

7.55 Put duck in hot serving
dish, arrange lemon slices
round (but do not add the
watercress until just before
serving). Add butter and
parsley to potatoes and
dish up.

8.00 Serve first course.

Fresh haddock mousse

1 lb fresh haddock fillet
salt
6 peppercorns
lemon juice

For mousse
$\frac{1}{2}$ pint milk
1 slice of onion
1 bayleaf
6 peppercorns
1 oz butter
1 teaspoon paprika pepper
$\frac{3}{4}$ oz flour

scant $\frac{1}{2}$ oz gelatine (soaked in
    3-4 tablespoons water — see
    page 152
3 tablespoons double cream
1 egg white

To finish
$\frac{1}{4}$ pint mayonnaise (see page 154)
1-2 tablespoons tomato juice (canned)
dash of Tabasco sauce
slices of tomato, or cucumber

Plain, or fish-shaped, mould
    (1$\frac{1}{2}$ pints capacity)

Method

Set oven at 350°F or Mark 4.

Wash and skin the fillet and place it in a puttered ovenproof dish with the seasoning and lemon juice. Cover dish with a buttered paper and cook, in pre-set moderate oven, for about 12-15 minutes. Allow fish to cool. Oil the mould lightly.

To prepare mousse : heat the milk with the onion, bayleaf and peppercorns, and infuse until it is well flavoured, then strain. Melt the butter, add the paprika pepper and cook for 1 minute ; remove pan from the heat, blend in the flour and the strained milk. Stir sauce until it is boiling, then tip it into a bowl ; cover and allow to cool.

Strain the fish and pound it in a bowl, adding cold sauce a little at a time. Dissolve gelatine over gentle heat, add to fish mixture.

Lightly whip the cream and stiffly whisk the egg white. Fold these into the fish mixture, turn into mould, leave to set.

Turn out mousse on to a serving dish. Coat with the mayonnaise, thinned slightly with the tomato juice and flavoured with Tabasco sauce. Garnish with slices of tomato or cucumber.

Turning the haddock mousse mixture into the oiled fish mould before leaving it to set

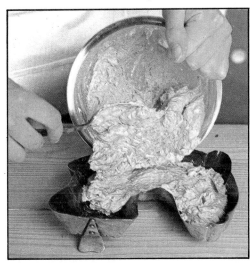

Roast duck Hymettus

1 large duck (about 5 lb dressed
   weight)
1 teaspoon oil
salt
1 onion (not peeled)
$\frac{1}{2}$ oz butter
2 tablespoons clear honey
juice of $\frac{1}{2}$ lemon
1 tablespoon arrowroot (mixed
   with 2 tablespoons water)

For garnish
$\frac{1}{2}$ bunch of watercress
1 lemon (sliced)

For stuffing
1 oz butter
1 medium-size onion (chopped)
4 oz walnut kernels, or cashew
   nuts (chopped)
4 oz fresh breadcrumbs
   grated rind of 1 lemon
1 tablespoon chopped parsley
1 teaspoon chopped sage
1 teaspoon chopped thyme,
   or marjoram
$\frac{1}{2}$ teaspoon cinnamon
salt and pepper
1 egg (beaten)
juice of $\frac{1}{2}$ lemon

Method

Brown the giblets, but not the liver, in 1
teaspoon oil, cover with 1 pint cold water,
bring to the boil and skim well. Season with
salt and 1 onion (washed and trimmed but
not peeled) and simmer gently for 30-45
minutes. Strain to make stock.

To prepare the stuffing: melt half the
butter, add the onion and cook slowly until
soft but not coloured, drop the remaining
butter into the pan and, when melted, add
the nuts and fry until golden-brown. Turn
the nuts and onions into a bowl, add the
rest of the ingredients and mix well. Stuff
into the body of the duck and truss neatly.

Rub the $\frac{1}{2}$ oz butter over the duck and
then spread with the honey. Roast in pre-set
oven at 375°F or Mark 5 for $1\frac{1}{2}$ hours (15
minutes per lb and 15 minutes over),
basting and turning from time to time.

Take up the duck, remove the trussing
strings, trim the leg and wing joints and set
on the serving dish.

Tip off the fat, leaving any sediment at the
bottom of the pan, add the strained lemon
juice and stock. Bring to the boil, season
well and thicken with the arrowroot.

Garnish the duck with watercress and
lemon slices, and serve with the gravy.

Note : new potatoes, boiled and tossed in
a little butter and chopped parsley, are best
with duck. For a vegetable, serve frozen
sliced green beans as described, right.

1 lb packet of sliced, or whole,
  frozen haricot beans
4 rashers of back bacon
½ oz butter
1 medium-size onion (finely
  chopped)
black pepper (ground from mill)

Method

Cook the beans as instructions on the packet : drain and refresh them with cold water. Drain well. Remove the rind and rust from the bacon and cut into ½-inch strips, set aside. Melt the butter in a sauté pan, add the onion and cook slowly until soft but not coloured, then add the bacon to the pan, increase the heat and fry until the bacon is crisp and the onion brown. Tip the beans into the pan and toss until hot, adding black pepper from the mill.

Savarin Chantilly

4½ oz flour
pinch of salt
¼ oz yeast (fresh or dried)
½ oz sugar
1 wineglass warm milk
2 eggs (beaten)
1¾ oz butter
¼ pint double cream (whipped,
    sweetened and flavoured with
    vanilla)
syrup (for basting) — see right

6-inch diameter savarin, or ring, mould

Method
Sift the flour and salt into a
warm bowl. Cream the yeast and
sugar together in the milk and
add to the flour with the beaten
eggs. Beat vigorously with your
hand for 5 minutes (see photo-
graphs, below). Cover the bowl
and leave in a warm place for
45-60 minutes until well risen.

Cream the butter until soft
and beat into the dough for 5
minutes. Well butter the savarin,
or ring, mould, pour in the
mixture and leave to prove for
5-10 minutes in a warm temperature.

Bake in oven at 400°F or Mark
6 until golden-brown (about 25
minutes).

Turn savarin out carefully on
to a cooling rack; while still
warm, baste with a moderately
heavy syrup. The savarin must
be well soaked and should
glisten with the syrup. For serving,
fill the middle of the savarin with
whipped cream.

*1 Beating eggs vigourously by hand
into the flour and yeast mixture*
*2 Taking the creamed butter to beat
into the dough after it has risen well*
*3 Pouring mixture into the buttered
savarin mould, before leaving it to
prove for 5-10 minutes before baking*
*4 (Right), the finished dish filled
in the middle with whipped cream*

Syrup for savarin

Dessert

Above : basting the cooked savarin with the flavoured syrup ; spoon back any syrup that runs on to plate

4 oz lump sugar
¼ pint water
2 thinly pared strips of lemon
  rind, or ½ vanilla pod (split)
kirsch, or rum (optional)

Method

Add sugar to the water, boil slowly to dissolve, then add lemon (or vanilla) and boil rapidly until **cooled** syrup is sticky between fingers (about 5 minutes). This syrup should be used while hot. It is usual to add kirsch or rum to flavour a savarin immediately before pouring over the syrup.

Potage madrilène

2 **pints strong chicken stock
   (cold) — see page 151**
1 **medium-size onion (finely
   chopped)**
1 **oz butter**
1 **large can (1 lb 12 oz) Italian plum
   tomatoes**
**bouquet garni (containing a strip of
   lemon rind)**
salt
6 **black peppercorns**
2 **glasses sherry**
1 **tablespoon arrowroot (mixed
   with 2 tablespoons water)**
squeeze of lemon juice
1 **small carton (3 fl oz) single
   cream**
1 **tablespoon chives (snipped)**

Although this recipe is not for a clarified soup (ie. consommé), it is nevertheless important to have it as free from fat as possible and that is why the chicken stock should be cold. It is only possible to get rid of every bit of grease from chicken stock if it is at refrigerator temperature.

Potage madrilène served in soup cups with a garnish of cream and fresh chives to give a party touch

Method

Skim the stock thoroughly. Cook the onion slowly in the butter in a pan until soft but not coloured, add the stock, tomatoes and bouquet garni and season well with salt and peppercorns. Stir until boiling, crushing the tomatoes well with wooden spoon, cover and simmer for 40 minutes. Pass through a Mouli sieve or rub through a nylon strainer. **Watchpoint** These methods are better than using an electric blender, as the latter breaks down the seeds. Both flavour and appearance are improved if the seeds are removed by straining.

Return the soup to the rinsed-out pan, boil the sherry until reduced to half and add to soup. Thicken very slightly with the arrowroot - this is done just to bind in the small amount of butter and to give a certain smoothness on the palate. Re-boil, add lemon juice and adjust the seasoning.

A spoonful of cream should be floated on top of each soup cup or plate as it is served; sprinkle with fresh snipped chives.

Menu 13 Duck

Starter : Greek lemon soup
Alternative : Whitings Orly with Sweet pimiento sauce

Main course : Ballotine of duck with Braised celery

Dessert : Apple mousse gâtinaise

TIMETABLE

Day before
Prepare and make apple
mousse, and poach remaining
apples separately.
Make greek lemon soup, but
do not add liaison. Make egg
white garnish. (Make the
fritter batter for whitings,
cover and put in refrigerator.
Prepare sweet pimiento sauce.)
Make breadcrumbs for duck
Make sauce for duck, cover
and keep in larder or cool
place.

Morning
Make stuffing.
Stuff duck and sew up.
If serving soup chilled, reheat,
add liaison, then cool and
place in refrigerator. (Skin
whiting and sprinkle with
lemon juice. Cover and leave
in refrigerator.)
Assemble ingredients and
equipment for final cooking
from 6.30 for dinner
around 8 pm.

Order of work

6.15 Set oven for duck.

6.30 Put duck into oven.
Prepare the 'toffee'
walnuts and decorate the
apple mousse gâtinaise.

6.50 Baste duck.

7.10 Turn and baste duck.
Cook potatoes.

7.15 Dry the whiting pieces
and then dip into batter
and deep-fry them. Leave
ready to serve and keep
warm.)

7.30 Baste duck. Cook
mushrooms.

7.45 If serving soup hot, reheat
it and add liaison. Garnish
ready to serve.
Dish up duck (being boned
it can be sliced at table
because the carving is so
easy). Keep warm.

8.00 Serve first course.

Greek lemon soup (Avgolemono)

thinly pared rind and juice of 1 small lemon
good oz butter
3 shallots (finely chopped)
1 rounded tablespoon flour
2 pints jellied chicken stock (see page 151)
2-3 egg yolks
3-4 tablespoons double cream (lightly
    whipped)

For garnish
1 egg white
1-2 tablespoons cream, or top of the milk
salt and pepper

This soup may be served hot or chilled.

Method

Melt butter in a pan, add chopped shallots
cover and cook very slowly for 2-3 minutes,
but do not allow them to colour. Draw pan
aside, stir in the flour, blend in the stock
and bring to the boil. Simmer for 10
minutes, then add the thinly pared rind of
the lemon and the strained juice.

Watchpoint Care must be taken that this
soup is not too sharp in flavour. To prevent
this, add the lemon juice to taste.

Continue to simmer the soup for a further
7-10 minutes. Then strain liquid, return to
the rinsed-out pan and draw aside.

Meanwhile set the oven at 325°F or Mark
3. Lightly beat the egg white for the garnish
with a fork just to break it, add the cream (or
milk) with the seasoning. Turn into an
individual soufflé dish or cocotte. Bake this
in pre-set oven for 7-10 minutes, or until
firm to the touch, leave until cold and turn
put, slice and cut out into tiny rounds, or
diamonds.

Mix the egg yolks together, add a little
of the warm soup, then add this mixture to
the soup as a liaison. Reheat, stirring
constantly, but do not allow to boil. Then
add the lightly whipped cream and the egg
white garnish just before serving. If serving
soup chilled, after adding liaison cool it and
put in refrigerator. The garnish should not
be added until just before serving.

Starter

Cutting the cold, cooked egg white into diamonds to garnish the soup

Ballotine of duck

1 duck (weighing 3-4 lb)
2 tablespoons cooking oil
1 glass dry sherry
$\frac{1}{4}$ lb button mushrooms (sliced)
$\frac{1}{2}$ oz butter

For stuffing
1 oz butter
1 onion (finely chopped)
12 oz pork, or veal (minced)
1 teacup of fresh breadcrumbs (see page 150)
1 dessertspoon parsley (chopped)
1 teaspoon dried sage
1 glass dry sherry
3 oz ham (shredded)
8 pistachio nuts (blanched and shredded) — see page 155

For sauce
2 tablespoons cooking oil
1 tablespoon carrot (finely diced)
1 tablespoon onion (finely diced)
$\frac{1}{2}$ tablespoon celery (finely diced)
1 rounded tablespoon flour
$\frac{3}{4}$ pint stock
few mushroom stalks, or peelings
1 teaspoon tomato purée
salt and pepper
bouquet garni

Trussing needle; fine thread, or string

Method

Ask your butcher to bone out the duck. Set the oven at 400°F or Mark 6.

To prepare the stuffing : melt the butter in a pan, add the onion and cook until soft but not coloured. Add to the minced meat and breadcrumbs and mix well with herbs, sherry, ham and pistachios. Bind with the beaten egg and season. Stuff the duck, sew up neatly with fine string and tie at intervals of 1-2 inches.

Heat 2 tablespoons oil in a roasting tin, set the duck on a grid in the tin and baste with the hot oil. Roast in pre-set oven for 1-1$\frac{1}{4}$ hours. Baste every 20 minutes and turn the bird after 40 minutes.

To prepare the sauce ; heat the oil in a pan, add the vegetables and when soft but not coloured, stir in the flour and cook slowly to a rich russet-brown.

Draw pan aside, pour on $\frac{1}{2}$ pint of stock, add all the other ingredients and then stir until boiling. Simmer very gently, with lid half on, for 20-30 minutes. Add half remaining cold stock, skim sauce well, simmer for a further 5 minutes. Repeat this process with the rest of the cold stock, then strain.

Cook the button mushrooms in the $\frac{1}{2}$ oz butter until soft. Take up duck, pour off fat and deglaze the roasting tin with the sherry. Strain and add to the sauce with the cooked mushrooms.

Serve the duck whole or sliced, pour over a little of the sauce and serve the rest of it separately.

As duck is quite a rich meat, choose boiled potatoes (preferably new ones) as an accompanying vegetable. Braised celery is a good second vegetable (see right).

Braised celery

Main course

3 **large heads of celery**
1 **large onion (diced)**
1 **large carrot (diced)**
1 **oz butter**
$\frac{1}{2}$ **pint jellied stock**
salt and pepper
bouquet garni

Method

Wash celery, split the heads in two, blanch in boiling salted water and drain.

Dice the onion and carrot, sweat them in butter in a pan (see method, page 88). Then add celery, stock, seasoning and bouquet garni. Cover and braise for 1-1$\frac{1}{2}$ hours or until tender in the oven at 325°F or Mark 3. Baste well from time to time.

When cooked, the gravy should be well reduced and the celery glazed. Dish up and strain gravy over celery.

Apple mousse gâtinaise

2½-3 lb dessert apples (Laxton,
   Cox, Blenheim, or Pippin,
   variety)
1½ oz unsalted butter
grated rind of ½ lemon
2-3 tablespoons thick honey
½ oz gelatine (dissolved in 2½ oz
   water and a squeeze of lemon
   juice) — see page 152
½ pint double cream
12, or more, walnut kernels
   (halved)
¾-1 pint sugar syrup (made with
   3-4 oz granulated sugar and ½-¾ pint
   water)

8½-9 inch diameter moule à manqué

This is so called because honey from Gâtinais, in the Orléans region, is well known all over France.

Method

Lightly oil the mould. Peel and core two-thirds of the apples, then grate or chop them. Rub ½ oz of the butter round a shallow pan, put in the apples and cook slowly to bring out the juice, then increase the heat and cook them rapidly to a pulp, stirring occasionally. Add the lemon rind and continue to cook until apples are a thick purée.

Draw pan aside, add honey to taste and, when this is melted, add the dissolved gelatine. Set pan aside to cool. When almost cold, partially whip the cream, just enough to hold its shape. Carefully fold this into the mixture and turn at once into the prepared mould. Leave until set.

Have the sugar syrup ready-made (see page 155, Poaching fruit). Peel the remainder of the apples (about 2-3), quarter and core them; poach in the sugar syrup until tender (for about 7-10 minutes). Leave to cool in the syrup with the lid on the pan. This will help them to become translucent. Drain the apples, reserving syrup, and set aside.

Put the remaining butter into the syrup and boil rapidly until reduced to a caramel. Stop further boiling by dipping the bottom of the pan into cold water, then drop in the walnut halves, turning them round quickly; lift them out on to an oiled tin or baking sheet. To dish up, turn out the mousse, arrange apple quarters on top or round the sides and decorate with 'toffee' walnuts.

Below : coating walnuts with caramel to make 'toffee' walnuts for mousse

108

Dessert

The apple mousse gâtinaise is decorated with 'toffee' walnuts and apple

Whitings Orly

3-4 whitings (about 12 oz filleted)
squeeze of lemon juice
seasoned flour
½-¾ pint fritter batter (see page 152)
deep fat (for frying)

Method

Skin the fillets, lay them on a plate and sprinkle lightly with a little lemon juice. Leave in the refrigerator for about 1 hour. Then dab the fillets with absorbent paper to dry and cut each one into diagonal strips about 1 inch or more in width.

To fry the whiting, first roll them in seasoned flour. Have the batter ready. Heat the fat bath until at frying temperature (see page 151). To test heat if you have no thermometer, drop in 1-inch cube of bread; it should turn golden-brown in 20 seconds in oil, and 40 seconds in solid fats. Put a few pieces of the fish into the batter. Turn round lightly with a flat whisk or fork, lift out and drop carefully into the fat. Fry about 6-8 pieces at a time; when golden-brown, lift out and drain on absorbent paper or a cooling rack set over a baking sheet, then set aside. Continue until all the pieces of fish are fried. Serve a sweet pimiento sauce separately.

Sweet pimiento sauce

2 egg yolks
1 hard-boiled egg yolk (sieved)
½ teaspoon paprika pepper
salt and pepper
dash of Tabasco sauce
grated rind of ½ orange
7½ fl oz olive, or salad, oil
about 1 dessertspoon vinegar
2 small caps of canned pimiento
— finely chopped, or sieved
1 tablespoon pimiento juice
1 tablespoon double cream

Method

Put the egg yolks, both raw and hard-boiled, into a bowl. Work with the seasonings and orange rind, then gradually add the oil as if making mayonnaise. When it begins to get too thick, add the vinegar. When all the oil is mixed in, add the chopped strained pimientos. Finish with juice from the can and the cream, if used, and adjust seasoning.

Menu 14 Fish

Starter : Avocado pear
Alternative : Potage Darblay

Main course : Sole Joinville

Dessert : Coffee meringue cake

TIMETABLE

Day before
Make coffee meringue cake and butter cream ; fill and finish, then dish up and leave in a cool place.

Morning
(Prepare and sieve soup. Cut and cook the garnish).
Prepare panade of fish, line and fill mould, cover with buttered paper or foil, cover and keep in refrigerator until the evening. Make fish stock (fumet) from sole bones for sauce.
Shell tail ends of prawns and make prawn butter.
Wash and trim mushrooms for sole Joinville.

Assemble ingredients and equipment for final cooking from 6.30 for dinner around 8 pm.

Order of work

6.30 Set oven at 325°F or Mark 3.

6.45 Put fish mould in bain-marie and put in oven to cook. Make velouté sauce, put in double saucepan over heat to keep warm.

7.00 Prepare avocados and put in refrigerator.

7.25 Put prawns in oven.
(Put soup on to heat but do not boil).
Cook mushrooms for sole Joinville.
Turn gas oven to lowest setting, electric oven off. Put plates and dishes to warm.

7.30 Turn fish on to serving dish but do not remove mould. Replace in oven.
(Put potatoes and French beans to cook, if serving).

7.45 Beat prawn butter into the velouté sauce.
(Dish up beans and potatoes).
Remove mould from fish, coat with sauce and garnish.

8.00 Serve first course.

111

Avocado pear

½ avocado per person
½-1 green pepper (enough to give
    2 tablespoons, chopped)
2 tablespoons spring onion
    (chopped)
6 black olives (stoned and
    shredded)

For vinaigrette dressing
salt
black pepper (ground from mill)
1½ tablespoons white wine
    vinegar
5 tablespoons salad oil
squeeze of lemon
caster sugar (to taste)
1 teaspoon parsley (chopped)

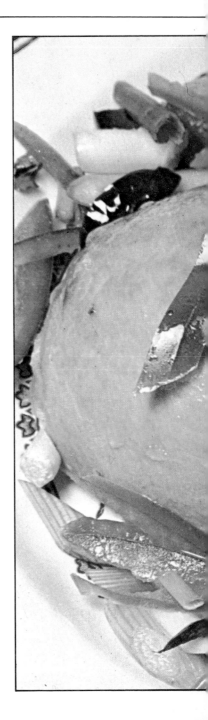

For a delicious and easy to prepare first course, serve avocado pears. Choose ripe ones, allowing one half per person. When ripe the fruit is slightly soft, and if shaken the stone will rattle a little. You can buy avocados a day or two before needed and leave to ripen in the dark (in the larder), but take the advice of your greengrocer on their state of ripeness.

Method

Drop the chopped green pepper into boiling water, cook for 1 minute, then drain and rinse well with cold water.

To make dressing : mix a large pinch of salt and black pepper with the vinegar and whisk in the oil. Sharpen with lemon juice and add a little sugar to taste. Add all other ingredients to this dressing.

Split the pears in half with a stainless steel or silver knife and remove the stone. Fill each half with the sharp vinaigrette dressing and chill slightly before serving on individual plates, or prepare as illustration.

Sole Joinville

4 slip soles (filleted, plus bones for stock)
$1\frac{1}{2}$ lb whiting, or hake, or 1 lb fresh haddock fillet
bouquet garni
1 carrot (sliced)
1 onion (sliced)
2 eggs (beaten)
5 tablespoons double cream
salt and pepper

For panade
$2\frac{1}{2}$ oz flour
2 oz butter
$\frac{3}{4}$ cup milk

For velouté sauce
1 oz butter
1 rounded tablespoon flour
$\frac{3}{4}$ cup fish stock (see method, below)
5 tablespoons single cream, or top of milk

For garnish
12 large prawns (unshelled)
$\frac{1}{2}$ lb button mushrooms
1 oz butter

For prawn butter
tail shells from prawns
1 oz unsalted butter

7-inch diameter savarin, or ring, mould

Method

Well grease the mould and set oven at 325°F or Mark 3.

Trim the fillets of sole, remove skin, wash and dry fillets thoroughly and leave wrapped in a cloth or absorbent paper until wanted. Skin and bone the whiting, hake or haddock and pass twice through a mincer. Check the weight of minced fish - you must have at least 12 oz but not more than 1 lb.

Make the stock by putting fish bones into a pan, adding water to cover and bouquet garni, sliced carrot and onion. Bring to boil and simmer gently for about 30 minutes, then strain and set aside.

To prepare the panade: sift $2\frac{1}{2}$ oz flour on to a piece of paper and set aside. Cut the 2 oz butter in pieces, put in a pan, add milk and bring slowly to the boil. Draw the pan off the heat and at once tip in all the sifted flour. Heat until smooth, turn on to a plate and leave to cool. Work the panade, beaten eggs and minced fish together and when thoroughly mixed and quite smooth, stir in the double cream and season well.

Line the savarin, or ring, mould with the fillets of sole, skinned side uppermost, overlapping slightly so that there are no gaps. Fill this lined mould with the fish panade and fold the ends of the fillets over the top. Cover with a piece of thickly-buttered greaseproof paper and cook au bain-marie in the pre-set oven for 40-45 minutes or until the fillets of sole are firm to the touch.

Meanwhile prepare garnish and prawn butter: peel away the tail shells only of the prawns; put the prawns between two buttered plates and set aside for heating. Trim and wash the mushrooms and put in a small pan with $\frac{1}{2}$ oz butter and seasoning.

Pound the prawn tail shells with 1 oz butter until smooth. This is best done with a pestle and mortar, but failing this, use the end of a rolling pin in a small basin. Rub this prawn butter through a strainer and set aside.

Now make velouté sauce: melt the butter in a pan, add the flour, cook gently to a pale straw colour, draw pan aside and blend in the stock. Return pan to the heat, stir until the sauce begins to thicken, then add the cream and bring to the boil. Cook for 2-3 minutes, draw aside and beat in the prawn butter, a small piece at a time. Taste and adjust the seasoning.

Put the prawns into the oven for 5 minutes to heat through; sauté the mushrooms quickly for 1 minute.

Turn the mould on to a hot serving dish and leave for 2-3 minutes. Then lift mould carefully and wipe up any juice that may come away from the fish with a clean cloth or absorbent paper. Then coat with the velouté sauce before filling the centre with the mushrooms; garnish with prawns.

This dish doesn't really need any accompanying vegetables, particularly when it is preceded by a starter.

Coffee meringue cake

4 egg whites
8 oz caster sugar

For butter cream
4 oz granulated sugar
5 tablespoons water
4 egg yolks
$\frac{3}{4}$ lb unsalted butter

1 teaspoon instant coffee
(dissolved in 2 teaspoons
hot water)

For decoration
3 oz browned almonds (finely
chopped) — see page 155
2 tablespoons icing sugar

Method

Have ready three baking sheets lined with non-stick (kitchen) paper and set the oven at 300°F or Mark $\frac{1}{2}$-1. (These are the best temperatures for electric and gas ovens, respectively.)

To make meringue : whish the egg whites in a bowl until stiff, add 4 teaspoons of the measured sugar and continue whisking for about 30 seconds. Fold in the remaining sugar with a metal spoon. Divide the mixture evenly between the three tins and spread carefully into rounds 8-9 inches in diameter. Bake in pre-set oven for about 50-60 minutes until meringue is dry and crisp. Leave to cool.

To prepare the butter cream ; dissolve the sugar in the water over gentle heat, then boil steadily to the thread (to test, cool a little on a spoon and **when it is cool** pull between finger and thumb to a fine thread). It is not necessary to use a sugar thermometer for this as a degree or two either way makes no difference to the butter cream.

Pour the syrup while still hot on to egg yolks, whisk until a thick mousse is formed. Cream the butter until soft and beat in the egg and sugar mousse a little at a time. Add sufficient coffee to give a good flavour.

When the meringue rounds are quite cold spread with some of the coffee butter cream and sandwich them together. Spread the top and sides with remaining butter cream and cover with almonds.

Cut four strips of greaseproof paper 1-inch wide and lay across the top of the cake ; the spaces between the strips should be the same. Dust the top of the cake with icing sugar, then carefully lift off each strip of paper.

Dessert

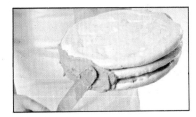

When the meringue rounds are cold, sandwich together with cream and spread rest on top and sides. Decorate with almonds and icing sugar

Potage Darblay

1 lb potatoes (peeled and thinly
sliced)
1 medium-size onion (thinly
sliced)
$1\frac{1}{2}$ oz butter
1 pint milk
$\frac{1}{2}$ pint water
$\frac{1}{2}$ bayleaf
salt and pepper

For garnish
1 medium-size carrot (cut in
julienne strips)
1 medium-size onion (cut in
julienne strips)
1 stick of celery (cut in julienne
strips)
1 oz butter
salt and pepper

For liaison
1 egg yolk
1 teaspoon arrowroot
4 tablespoons single cream

Method

Melt $1\frac{1}{2}$ oz butter in a pan, add the sliced potatoes and onion and stir. Press a buttered paper on the vegetables, cover with the lid and cook very slowly for 6 minutes. Pour on the milk and water, add bayleaf and seasoning and bring to the boil. Cover pan and simmer for 20 minutes.

Watchpoint Do not put the lid on your pan until you have made quite sure that the soup is only simmering very gently. If your stove is difficult to regulate to a very low heat, it would be wise to leave the lid of the pan lifted at one side, as milk rises in the pan so quickly. If you do have an accident, stop and wipe both pan and stove immediately.

To prepare the garnish: use the red part only of the carrot (not the woody core) and cut this, the onion and celery into julienne strips (for this garnish they should be no longer than $1\frac{1}{2}$ inches). Melt the butter in a small pan, add the vegetables, season lightly and stir. Cover with a buttered paper and a close-fitting lid and cook gently for 8-10 minutes.

Watchpoint The vegetables for the garnish must not colour. As the carrot takes longest to cook, test this with the point of a knife to make sure it is tender. These vegetables can instead be cooked for 3 minutes on top of the stove, then put in a casserole in the oven at 350°F or Mark 4 for 12 minutes or until tender.

Pass the soup through a Mouli sieve or wire sieve, or purée in an electric liquidiser. Return the soup to a clean pan, whisk well to make sure the purée is even and bring to the boil.

To prepare liaison: mix the egg yolk with the arrowroot and cream and add about 2 tablespoons of hot soup to it. Draw the rest of the soup to one side and slowly pour in the liaison, stirring all the time.

Reheat very carefully and slowly so that the soup only just comes to boiling point; add the garnish and serve.

Menu 15 Fish

Starter : Asparagus with melted butter, or Hollandaise sauce
Alternative : Cream of asparagus soup

Main course : Salmon (sea) trout en gelée, Mayonnaise Nantua

Dessert : Strawberry japonais

TIMETABLE

Day before
Make almond meringue
rounds and store in an airtight
container.
Cook the salmon trout, but
do not skin ; keep covered
in a cool place.
Make aspic jelly and keep
covered in a cool place.

Morning
Prepare asparagus and tie in
bundles for boiling (or make
the asparagus soup, but do
not add the liaison).
Scrape new potatoes, leave
in pan of cold water.
Skin salmon trout, dish up
and coat with aspic ; prepare
the salmon garnish. Pound
prawn shells, soak them in
oil and make the mayonnaise
Nantua.
Prepare coffee-flavoured
icing and ice one round of
the japonais.

Assemble ingredients and
equipment for final cooking
from 7 for dinner around
8 pm.

Order of work

7.00 Whip cream, slice the
strawberries and dust with
sugar ; fill the japonais.

7.30 Put potatoes and asparagus on to cook.

7.45 Drain asparagus, dish up
and keep warm. Melt
butter. (Reheat soup and
add liaison ; keep warm.)
Drain potatoes, dry and
leave in pan with a folded
napkin on top to absorb
the steam ; keep them
warm.

8.00 Serve first course.
Drop butter and parsley
into hot pan when ready
to finish the new potatoes.

Asparagus with melted butter

1-2 **bundles of asparagus**
4 **oz butter**

Method

Trim the bottom stalks of the asparagus, leaving about 2-3 inches before the green starts. To make sure that all stalks are the same length, cut them while asparagus is still tied in bundles. After untying them, rinse stalks well in cold water and then, using a small vegetable knife, scrape the white part of the stems well and stand them in a bowl of cold water. Now tie the spears together in bundles, according to size, with fine string; leave the cut stems standing in cold water until you are ready to cook them.

Have ready a deep pan of plenty of boiling salted water and stand the asparagus spears in this, stalk end down; cook gently, covered, for 12-15 minutes or until the green part is tender.

Watchpoint The green tips should stand above the water and cook just in the steam.

Lift spears carefully from the pan, drain them well on clean muslin and then place them on a folded napkin in a hot serving dish. Cut and remove the string from each bundle. Melt the butter gently in a small pan, but do not let it get too hot and oily. Then skim it well and pour into a hot sauce boat and serve separately.

Note : If you wish to serve asparagus as a starter to a main course which has a less rich sauce than that which is served with the salmon trout, you may wish to serve asparagus with hollandaise sauce (see right).

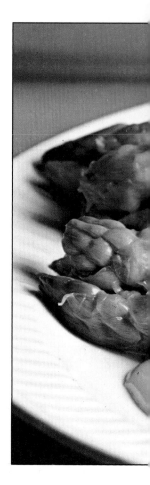

Hollandaise sauce

Put 4 tablespoons wine vinegar into a small pan with 6 peppercorns, 1 blade of mace, 1 slice of onion and $\frac{1}{2}$ bayleaf. Boil this liquid until it is reduced to a scant tablespoon, then set pan aside.

Cream 3 egg yolks in a bowl with a good $\frac{1}{2}$ oz butter and a pinch of salt. Strain the vinegar mixture on to this, set the bowl over a pan of boiling water. Turn off the heat under the pan, then add $4\frac{1}{2}$ oz butter in small pieces to the egg mixture, stirring vigorously all the time.

Watchpoint When you add the butter, it should be slightly soft, not straight from the refrigerator.

When all the butter has been added and the sauce is thick, taste for seasoning and add 1-2 tablespoons of cream (or top of the milk) and a squeeze of lemon juice (optional). Pleasantly sharp yet bland, the sauce should have the consistency of thick cream.

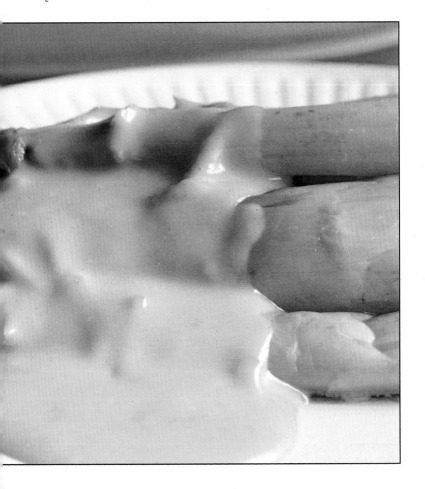

Salmon (sea) trout en gelée

2½-3 lb salmon trout
2 oz gelatine (see page 152)
1 tablespoon white wine vinegar
2½ fl oz sherry
2 egg whites

For court bouillon
1 carrot (sliced)
1 onion (stuck with a clove)
bouquet garni
4 peppercorns
1½ tablespoons vinegar
1½ pints water
salt

For garnish
½ pint prawns
½ cucumber
1 bunch of watercress

Method

First make the court bouillon : put all ingredients in a pan and bring to the boil. Cover, simmer for 20 minutes and strain. Trim trout and vandyke the tail (see page 137). Wash fish well, taking care to scrape away the blood that lies against the backbone and to remove the gills (this may have been done by the fishmonger). Slightly curl the fish and place it, underside down, in a fish kettle or oven-proof dish and pour over the well-seasoned court bouillon while it is still warm. Poach fish for 25-30 minutes in a fish kettle, or poach in the oven for 35-45 minutes (set oven at 350°F or Mark 4). On no account must the liquid around the fish boil, and if poaching fish in oven baste it frequently.

Allow the fish to cool in the court bouillon, then lift it carefully on to a board or large dish. Use absorbent paper to remove any specks of fat floating on the surface of fish stock and strain it into a clean, scalded pan, ready for making the aspic.

To prepare aspic jelly : first dissolve gelatine in a little cold fish stock, then set pan of remaining fish stock on moderate heat and whisk it backwards and downwards (the reverse of the usual whisking movement), until stock is hot. Then add gelatine, sherry and egg whites ; continue whisking steadily until stock boils.

Stop whisking and allow liquid to rise to the top of the pan ; turn off the heat or draw pan aside and leave liquid to settle for about 5 minutes, then bring it again to the boil, draw pan aside once more and leave it to settle. At this point the liquid should look clear ; if not, repeat the boiling process.

Filter the aspic jelly through a clean cloth and allow it to cool before using.

Snip skin along top of trout and remove it carefully, leaving head and tail intact. Cut through the backbone just below head and ease knife along the bone ; gently lift bone up and out towards the tail ; cut it just short of the tail and discard it.

Run a little cool aspic over the serving dish and leave it to set. Lift the trout, using a fish slice and palette knife for support, and place it on the prepared dish.

Slice the cucumber finely ; peel the tail shells from the prawns but do not remove their heads. Arrange the prawns along the top of the fish and then baste with cold liquid aspic. Decorate the dish with the cucumber and watercress and serve with mayonnaise Nantua and new potatoes, tossed in melted butter and chopped parsley.

Mayonnaise Nantua

3 oz shrimps, or prawns (with shells)
½ pint olive oil
½ teaspoon paprika pepper
2-3 egg yolks
salt and pepper
about 1½-2 dessertspoons white wine vinegar (to taste)

Method

Shell the shrimps (or the prawns). Pound the shells with the paprika in the oil and leave to soak for 10-15 minutes. Chop the prawns roughly, or leave shrimps whole, and strain the oil.

To make mayonnaise: work egg yolks and seasonings with a small whisk or wooden spoon in a bowl until thick; then start adding the strained oil drop by drop (when 2 tablespoons of oil have been added, the mixture will be very thick). Now carefully stir in 1 teaspoon of the vinegar. Add the remaining oil more quickly; either 1 tablespoon at a time and beaten thoroughly between each addition until it is absorbed, or, if you are using an electric beater, in a thin, steady stream.

When all the oil is absorbed, add remaining vinegar to taste, extra seasoning, if necessary, and the shrimps (or prawns).

Strawberry japonais

3 oz ground almonds
6 oz caster sugar
3 egg whites
8 oz coffee-flavoured glacé icing
  (see page 152)
$\frac{1}{2}$ lb strawberries
$\frac{1}{4}$ pint double cream
1 oz ground almonds (browned) — see page 155

Method

Set oven at 275-325°F or Mark 1-3. Mix the 3 oz of ground almonds and 6 oz sugar together and pass them through a wire sieve or strainer to make sure they are thoroughly blended. Whisk the egg whites until stiff, then fold in the almond and sugar mixture.

Divide this meringue mixture in two and spread into 6-6$\frac{1}{2}$-inch rounds on two baking sheets lined with non-stick kitchen paper. Bake in pre-set oven for about 50-60 minutes and then lift almond meringue carefully on to a cooling rack; turn it over to peel off the kitchen paper and then leave it to cool.

Coat one round of the almond meringue with the coffee-flavoured icing. Reserve a few strawberries for decoration; slice the rest and dust them with a little caster sugar.

Lightly whip the cream, sweeten it with 1 teaspoon caster sugar and flavour with vanilla essence. Spoon the cream on to the plain round of japonais and cover with the sliced strawberries. Place the iced round on top of this filling and press the browned ground almonds around the sides. Decorate the top with the whole strawberries.

Top left : covering a round of japonais with the coffee-flavoured icing for top layer of cake
Top right : spooning sliced strawberries on to the plain round of japonais which has been covered with almond-flavoured whipped cream
Right : the strawberry japonais ready to serve

Cream of asparagus soup

2 bundles of sprue, or 1 bundle
  of asparagus
1½ pints of veal, or chicken, stock
1 small onion (finely chopped)
1 oz butter
¾ oz flour
salt and pepper

For liaison
2 egg yolks
1 small carton (about 3 fl oz)
  double cream

Method

Wash and trim the tied bundle
of sprue or asparagus (see page
120), then cut prepared stalks
into 1-inch pieces and put these
in a pan with the stock and
onion. Cover pan and simmer
until asparagus is tender; reserve a few of the tips for garnish.
Rub the soup through a nylon
sieve or work in a blender.

Rinse out the pan. Melt butter
in pan, blend in flour, then add
the sieved or blended liquid
and season. Bring this to the
boil, then simmer it for 2-3
minutes. Add this liaison to the
soup and reheat it carefully
(do not let it boil). Adjust
seasoning, add reserved asparagus tips and serve hot.

Menu 16 Veal

Starter : Prawns in aspic

Main course : Shoulder of veal hongroise, Cucumber Vichy

Dessert : Pears Charcot
Alternative : Apple chartreuse

TIMETABLE

Day before
Make fish stock.
(Make apple chartreuse, leave in mould in refrigerator).

Morning
Clarify aspic and make prawn moulds.
Poach pears in syrup, make vanilla cream and leave to set.
Make the sauce for pears.
Prepare tomatoes and pimientos. Crush garlic, mix with butter and paprika and spread on to meat.
Prepare potatoes.
Cut cucumber, blanch and refresh. Peel and cut carrots, put in pan with butter, sugar and water. Chop parsley and shallot.
(Make sauce for apple chartreuse or whip and mix cream).

Assemble ingredients and equipment for final cooking from 5.50 for dinner around 8 pm.

Order of work

5.50 Set oven and assemble serving dishes.

6.00 Put meat in oven.
Turn out prawns and garnish. Cut brown bread and butter to accompany prawns.
Keep covered.

6.15 Baste meat, and thereafter at 15-minute intervals.
Dish up pears Charcot.
(Remove chartreuse from mould and put on serving dish).

6.45 Turn meat and baste again.

7.10 Put carrots to cook. Add cucumber when water has evaporated.

7.30 Cook potatoes (or noodles). Take up meat, drain potatoes (or noodles).
Turn electric oven off, or gas oven low ; put plates to warm.
Carve meat, finish sauce and dish up.
Return meat to oven to keep warm.

8.00 Serve first course.

127

Prawns in aspic

4-6 oz prawns (shelled)
1¼ pints aspic jelly made with fish stock (see
page 158)
For garnish
pimiento
chervil
1 box of small cress
8 prawns

8 dariole, or castle, moulds

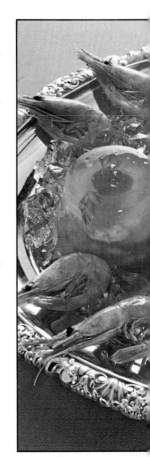

Method
Line the moulds with a thin coating of
cool aspic jelly, making a layer of about ¼
inch on the bottom of each one. Cut a small
round of pimiento for each mould, dip this
into a little aspic jelly and place it at the
bottom of each one. Put a small sprig of
chervil at each side of the pimiento rounds.
Cool 1 tablespoon aspic jelly at a time on a
cube of ice and run this on to the decoration
to hold it in position. Leave to set.

Arrange prawns and remaining aspic jelly
in layers until the moulds are full, finishing
with aspic. Pour any aspic left over into a
shallow tin to use for decoration; leave in a
cool place to set, then chop it roughly.

Allow at least 1-2 hours before turning
out prawns. If serving them on a silver or
steel dish, run a thin coating of cool aspic
over the bottom of the dish and leave it to
set. Unmould the prawns carefully by dipping
them in hot water and serve them on the
dish, garnished with small cress, chopped
aspic and the few reserved prawns; serve
them with brown bread and butter.

Top left : using a skewer when arranging the
pimiento and chervil in bottom of the moulds
Top right : layering prawns and aspic in moulds ;
stand them in a tray of ice when doing this in
order to quicken the cooling and setting process
Right : the finished dish, ready to be served

Shoulder of veal hongroise

2½ lb shoulder of veal (boned)
2 cloves of garlic (crushed)
1 dessertspoon paprika pepper
2 oz butter
1 bayleaf
1 shallot (finely chopped)
½-¾ pint veal, or chicken, stock (see pages 151, 158)
salt and pepper
3 tomatoes
2 caps of pimientos (canned)
1 tablespoon flour
2-3 tablespoons plain yoghourt

Method

Crush the garlic to a paste with the paprika and ½ oz of the butter. Then, with a sharp-pointed knife, make about 12 incisions over the surface of the joint. Work the paste well into these.

Heat remaining butter in a roasting tin in the oven set at 375°F or Mark 5, put in the meat and baste well. Add bayleaf, shallot, ½ pint stock and a little seasoning to the roasting tin and put in the oven for 1½ hours. Baste veal every 15 minutes, and turn it half way through the cooking time.

Scald and skin the tomatoes, cut in four, scoop out the seeds and then cut again. Slice the pimientos. Take up the meat, turn electric oven off or gas oven to its lowest setting.

Carve the meat and arrange in an entrée dish; keep warm. Strain the liquid from the roasting tin; measure and make up to ½ pint with extra stock or water, if necessary. Skim the fat from the top of the liquid, blend with the flour to make a smooth paste and mix into the stock in a saucepan. Stir until boiling, add the prepared tomato and pimiento and simmer for 2-3 minutes; taste for seasoning. Spoon this sauce over the meat.

Beat the yoghourt lightly with a fork and pour over the top of the meat. Cover the dish with a lid or foil and put back in the warm oven for 15-20 minutes.

Serve with noodles, or new potatoes and cucumber Vichy.

Cucumber Vichy

Main course

1 large cucumber
½ lb new carrots
½ oz butter
1 teaspoon sugar
large pinch of salt
1 dessertspoon chopped parsley
pepper (ground from mill)

Method

Peel the cucumber, cut in half lengthways and then across in ½-inch slices. Blanch in boiling salted water for 1 minute, then drain, refresh and set aside. Peel and quarter carrots and put in a pan with the butter, sugar, salt and enough water to cover. Cook until just tender (about 10 minutes) with the lid on.

Take the lid off the pan and continue cooking until the water has evaporated; add the prepared cucumber and parsley and season with pepper. Toss vegetables carefully until they are coated with the butter, sugar and parsley glaze.

Pears Charcot

4 ripe dessert pears
½ pint water
3 tablespoons sugar
juice of ½ lemon
2 tablespoons smooth apricot jam
½ lb quince jam

For vanilla cream
¾ pint milk
1 vanilla pod, or 2-3 drops of
  vanilla essence
3 egg yolks
2 tablespoons caster sugar
½ oz gelatine (softened in 5
  tablespoons water) — see page 152
¼ pint double cream (lightly
  whipped)

*Deep 5-6 inch diameter cake tin, or
  6-inch diameter top (No. 2 size)
  soufflé dish, or 8-inch diameter
  sandwich tin*

Method

Lightly oil the tin or soufflé dish. Put the water, sugar and lemon juice in a pan over gentle heat. When the sugar has dissolved, boil for 3 minutes. Meanwhile peel the pears, cut in half, scoop out the core with a teaspoon and immediately place pear halves, rounded side down, in the hot syrup. Cover the pan and poach pears carefully for 15-20 minutes; leave them to cool in the pan.

To make vanilla cream; heat the milk to scalding point with the vanilla pod (or vanilla essence), cover pan and leave milk to infuse until it is well flavoured. Cream egg yolks thoroughly with the sugar, and add the milk (first taking out the vanilla pod); blend liquid well, return it to the pan and stir over gentle heat until the custard coats the back of the wooden spoon, then strain and leave it to cool.

Melt the gelatine mixture over gentle heat, and add it to the custard. Tip the custard into a thin saucepan and stand this in a bowl of cold water (for quickness, add a little ice to water). Stir until custard begins to thicken creamily, then fold in half the whipped cream.

Turn the mixture into prepared tin or soufflé dish and leave to set (about 2 hours). Lift the pears out of the syrup and keep on one side; add the jams to the syrup in the pan, melt slowly and then boil for 2-3 minutes. Allow syrup sauce to cool.

Turn the vanilla cream on to a serving dish and decorate with the remaining cream. Arrange the pears round the cream and coat them with the sauce.

After scooping out centre of pears, place them, rounded side down, in the pan of hot syrup to poach

Apple chartreuse

1 large cooking apple
$\frac{1}{2}$ pint water
8 oz lump sugar
pared rind and strained juice of
    1 lemon
2 lb crisp dessert apples (Cox's
    Orange Pippin, or Russet, or
    Sturmer)
4 oz candied fruit (mixture of
    glacé cherry, angelica, pineapple,
    apricot and orange peel)
    — chopped

*6-inch diameter cake tin (1 $\frac{1}{2}$ pints
capacity), or 6-inch diameter top
(No. 2 size) soufflé dish*

Method

Wipe the cooking apple, remove the stalk and eye, cut in slices but do not remove the peel, core or pips. Put slices in a saucepan with the water, cover and simmer gently until pulpy. Tip into a nylon strainer, over a bowl, and leave undisturbed until all the juice has dripped through. Measure the amount of juice (you need $7\frac{1}{2}$ fl oz) and put this in a large shallow pan with the sugar, rind and lemon juice and set on a low heat. When all the sugar has dissolved, boil juice steadily for 5 minutes, draw pan aside and remove the lemon rind.

Peel and core the dessert apples and slice straight into the pan of juice - they must be cut very evenly and quite thinly ($\frac{1}{8}$ inch). Cover the pan and cook apples gently for 10-12 minutes. **Watchpoint** During this cooking time turn the apple slices once or twice, taking great care not to break them or let the syrup boil - it should just simmer very gently.

Take the lid off the pan and continue cooking until there is just enough syrup to moisten the apple slices. Draw off the heat, add the candied fruits, cover the pan and leave until the apples look clear. Tip into the wet cake tin or soufflé dish and leave in a cool place to set. (No gelatine is needed with this chartreuse as the natural pectin in the fruit is sufficient to set it.)

Turn chartreuse out of the tin or dish and serve with fresh cream or soured cream sauce, or a sharp rum and apricot sauce. We think the slightly sharp flavour of soured cream goes particularly well with this pudding.

Rum and apricot sauce

4 tablespoons smooth apricot jam
2 tablespoons water
juice of $\frac{1}{2}$ lemon
1 tablespoon rum

Method

Put jam, water and the lemon juice in a pan and heat gently to melt the jam. Bring sauce to the boil. Remove from the heat, add rum and strain sauce into a bowl. Serve cold.

Soured cream sauce

Take $\frac{1}{4}$ pint of fresh double cream, whip it until it begins to thicken, then stir in $\frac{1}{4}$ pint of soured cream and 1 teaspoon caster sugar.

Menu 17 Veal

Starter : Trout meunière
Alternative : Melon salad

Main course : Braised veal Orloff

Dessert : Almond and apricot flan

TIMETABLE

Day before
Make almond pastry, wrap in
greaseproof or waxed paper
and leave in refrigerator.
Poach the apricots, leave to
cool, then cover and keep in
a cool place. Cook veal and
soubise.

Morning
Line flan ring and bake pastry.
Carve veal, stuff and reshape.
Prepare mornay sauce and
coat meat. Prepare sprouts
and mushrooms. Drain
apricots, make glaze.
Wash and trim fish. Chop the
parsley and herbs. (Prepare
melon salad, cover and put in
refrigerator.)

Assemble ingredients and
equipment for final cooking
from 6.45 for dinner
around 8 pm.

Order of work

6.45 Whip cream and finish
apricot flan.
Set oven at 350°F or Mark
4 ; put plates and dishes
to warm.

7.00 Fry trout, dish up and
keep warm.

7.20 Put the meat into oven to
heat through.
Boil the rice. Cook sprouts
and mushrooms ; dish up
and keep warm.

7.50 Make meunière butter for
trout and serve at once.

Trout meunière

6 rainbow trout (2 extra for second helpings)
4 tablespoons flour (sifted with pinch of salt
   and pepper)
1½ oz butter

To finish
1 oz butter
juice of ½ lemon
salt and pepper
1 dessertspoon parsley (finely chopped)
1 teaspoon freshly chopped herbs (chives,
   thyme and chervil) - optional

Use fresh herbs when in season; but not
dried, mixed herbs because these would
spoil the flavour.

Method

Wash trout and check that they have been
cleaned thoroughly, then dry with absorbent
pager. Cut off fins and trim or 'vandyke' the
tails (see right). If the fish are large, score
them once or twice on either side and then
roll them in seasoned flour. Heat a heavy
frying pan, drop in 1½ oz butter and when
foaming put in the fish and cook until
golden-brown on either side, turning once
(about 12 minutes in all).

You will get better results with a heavy
frying pan as this can be heated before the
butter is put in the pan. In this way you can
get enough heat to start cooking the fish
before the butter browns. If a thin pan is
used, take extra care and start the cooking
with only 1 oz butter, add the rest when you
fry the last 2-3 fish. (If using a non-stick
frying pan, be sure to follow the manu-
facturer's instructions.)

Place the trout, without draining, on a hot
serving dish and keep warm. Wipe out the
frying pan with absorbent paper, add the
remaining butter and cook slowly until nut-
brown (to a noisette); add the lemon juice,
seasoning and herbs and while still foaming
pour over the trout. Serve at once.

The tails can either be trimmed neatly or 'vandyked' — tail line is accentuated by cutting a V-shape to make two distinct points as above

Before frying, roll fish in seasoned flour. When butter is foaming, put fish in the pan and cook until they are golden-brown on either side

Braised veal Orloff

$2\frac{1}{2}$ lb fillet of veal
1 oz butter
1 large onion (diced)
2 carrots (diced)
1 stick of celery (diced)
1 wineglass white wine
1 wineglass white wine
$\frac{1}{2}$ pint stock
salt and pepper
bouquet garni
1 rounded teaspoon arrowroot
   (mixed with 1 tablespoon cold
   water)

To garnish
8 oz mushrooms
$\frac{1}{4}$ oz butter
salt and pepper
squeeze of lemon juice

For soubise
2 large onions (chopped)
$\frac{1}{2}$ oz butter
3 oz Carolina rice
$\frac{1}{4}$ pint stock
salt and pepper
1 egg yolk
1 tablespoon cream

For mornay sauce
1 oz butter
1 rounded tablespoon flour
$\frac{1}{2}$ pint milk
2-3 tablespoons cheese (grated)
1 tablespoon cream

*Serve Braised veal Orloff with
boiled rice and brussels sprouts*

Method

Tie the veal neatly with string to keep it a good shape while cooking. Melt the butter in a flameproof casserole, add the diced vegetables and set the meat on top. Cover the dish and cook for 30 minutes in the oven at 350°F or Mark 4.

Pour over the white wine, cover the casserole again, return to the oven and continue cooking to reduce the wine (allow 30 minutes for this). Pour over the stock, which should come half-way up the meat, season, tuck in the bouquet garni by the meat and cover with greaseproof paper and the lid.

Lower the oven to 325°F or Mark 3 and cook the veal for 2 hours.

Meanwhile prepare the soubise, mornay sauce and garnish.

To prepare the soubise : cook the chopped onion gently in the butter until soft but not coloured, add the rice and stock and season. Bring to the boil, cover and cook in the oven for about 30 minutes, until very soft.

Watchpoint You must overcook rice so that each grain will split. Rub it through a wire strainer or mix to a purée in an electric blender. Then stir in the egg yolk and cream.

To prepare the mornay sauce ; melt butter, remove from heat, add the flour and blend in milk, then return to heat and stir until boiling. Cook for 2 minutes, cool, then gradually beat in the cheese and cream. Cover with a buttered greaseproof paper to prevent a skin forming.

Trim and wash the mushrooms and cook for 1-2 minutes in $\frac{1}{4}$ oz butter, salt and pepper and a squeeze of lemon.

Take veal out of oven and keep warm. Strain the stock from the veal in the pan and thicken lightly with the arrowroot mixture. Season and set aside for gravy.

Carve the meat, spread each slice with the soubise purée and reshape the joint on the serving dish. Spoon over the mornay sauce and brown in the oven at 400°F or Mark 6 for 12-15 minutes. Pour a little of the gravy round the meat and garnish with the mushrooms. Hand gravy separately.

Almond and apricot flan

1 lb fresh apricots
sugar syrup (made with $\frac{1}{2}$ pint water and
    3 tablespoons granulated sugar)
2 tablespoons apricot jam (sieved)
1 rounded teaspoon arrowroot (mixed with 1
    tablespoon water) - optional
$\frac{1}{4}$-$\frac{1}{2}$ pint double cream (whipped, sweetened
    with little caster sugar and flavoured with
    kirsch)
few almonds (blanched and split) — see page 155

For almond pastry
1 oz shortening
3 oz butter
6 oz plain flour
1$\frac{1}{2}$ oz ground almonds
1$\frac{1}{2}$ oz caster sugar
1 egg yolk
1-2 tablespoons cold water

8-inch diameter flan ring

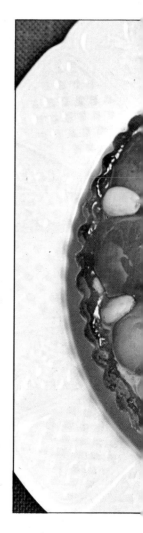

Method
Prepare sugar syrup for poaching the fruit.
Halve and stone apricots, and poach them
in the syrup until quite tender (see page 155).

Prepare the pastry. Rub the fats into the
flour, add the ground almonds and sugar.
Mix the egg yolk with water and add to the
dry ingredients. Work lightly to a firm dough
and chill slightly. Roll out, line into flan
ring and bake blind (see page 157) for about
10-15 minutes at 375°F or Mark 5. After
10 minutes, when pastry is firm, remove
paper and beans (used for baking blind) and
continue cooking for 3-5 minutes to dry
bottom of flan. Pastry should not colour.

Drain the apricots, boil the juice until
thick and syrupy, then add jam and stir until
melted. Strain and if glaze is too runny,
thicken with the slaked arrowroot; allow
this glaze to cool before using.

When flan case is quite cold, fill with
whipped cream, arrange the apricots and
almonds on top and brush with glaze.

Dessert

After poaching apricots, bake flan case; when quite cold, fill with whipped cream before arranging fruit

Melon salad

1 honeydew melon
1 lb tomatoes
1 large cucumber
salt
1 tablespoon parsley (chopped)
1 heaped teaspoon mint and
    chives (chopped)

For French dressing
2 tablespoons wine vinegar
salt and pepper
caster sugar
6 tablespoons salad oil

Method

Cut the melon in half, remove the seeds and scoop out the flesh with a vegetable cutter or cut into cubes.

Skin and quarter the tomatoes, squeeze out the seeds and remove the core; cut quarters again if the tomatoes are large.

Peel the cucumber, cut in small cubes, or the same size as the melon cubes. Sprinkle lightly with salt, cover with a plate and stand for 30 minutes; drain away any liquid and rinse cubes with cold water.

To prepare the dressing: mix the vinegar, seasoning and sugar together, whisk in oil.

Mix the fruit and vegetables together in a deep bowl (or soup tureen), pour over the dressing, cover and chill for 2-3 hours.

Just before serving, mix in the herbs. Serve from the bowl or tureeen with a ladle into soup cups.

While standing, the salad will make a lot of juice, so it should be eaten with a spoon.

Melon salad, an unusual starter

Menu 18 Veal

Starter : Salad Clémentine

Main course : Veal chops bonne femme, Courgettes au gratin

Dessert : Nusskuchen

TIMETABLE

Day before
Make and bake cake for
nusskuchen ; when cold keep
in airtight tin or polythene bag.
Prepare the filling for the cake.
Hardboil the eggs for salad
Clémentine.

Morning
Cook pork, cut into lardons
and blanch onions for veal
chops.
(Prepare soup and cool, but
do not add the top of the milk.)

Assemble equipment for
final cooking from 5.30 for
dinner around 8 pm.

Order of work

5.30 Prepare courgettes.
Skin tomatoes for the salad
Clémentine and sauté
them. Chop herbs ; soak
anchovies in milk ; prepare
dressing for the salad.
Split and fill cake and
finish with icing sugar or
chocolate. Cut brown bread
and butter.

6.45 Brown veal chops and
start to cook.

7.00 Put veal chops to simmer
and prepare potatoes.
Dish up salad Clémentine
and put in the refrigerator
to chill.

7.25 Put potatoes in with veal
chops. Cook courgettes
and prepare egg, cream
and cheese mixture for
them.

7.45 Dish up veal chops, leaving
parsley to be sprinkled on
before serving ; keep hot.
Put finished courgettes in
oven to brown gently.
(Reheat soup.)

8.00 Serve salad. (Add top of
milk to soup and serve.)

Salad Clémentine

6 tomatoes
salt and pepper
2 tablespoons salad oil
6 eggs (hard-boiled and sliced)
1 tablespoon capers
1 tablespoon gherkins (sliced)
6 anchovy fillets
brown bread and butter (for serving)

For dressing
2 tablespoons wine vinegar
1 teaspoon dry mustard
6 tablespoons salad oil
3 dessertspoons tomato ketchup
1 tablespoon mixed herbs (fresh parsley,
    chives and mint, or 1 tablespoon parsley and
    pinch of dried mixed herbs) — chopped
salt
black pepper (ground from mill)

Method

Scald and skin the tomatoes (see page 156)
cut in half through the stalk, cut out the
small piece of core at the stalk end and
remove seeds. Season tomatoes lightly.
Heat oil in a pan and sauté tomatoes very
quickly on each side ; lift them out very
carefully and leave to cool.

Peel and slice the eggs and arrange them
in the bottom of an entrée dish, scatter the
capers and gherkins over them. Set the
tomatoes, cut side downwards, on top.

Split the anchovies in half and soak them
in 2 tablespoons milk to remove excess salt.

Combine the ingredients for the dressing,
adding salt and black pepper to taste.

Drain the anchovy fillets and arrange them
lattice-wise over the tomatoes ; pour over
the dressing. Chill salad in refrigerator for
1 hour before serving with slices of brown
bread and butter.

Watchpoint Tomatoes, even if very ripe,
must be sautéd in the oil for this dish. If this
is not done they make too much juice when
standing after the dressing is poured on.

Starter

Decorate with anchovy fillets, capers and gherkins and coat with dressing

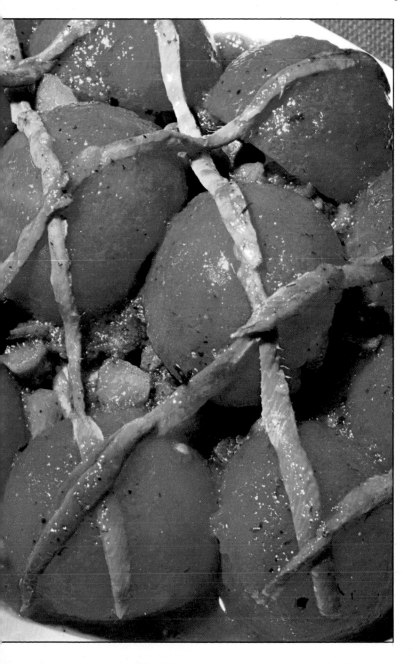

Veal chops bonne femme

4 veal chops
6 oz pickled belly pork, or 4 oz gammon
   rasher
16 button onions (peeled)
4 oz button mushrooms (halved, or quartered)
$1\frac{1}{2}$ oz butter
1 rounded tablespoon flour
1 wineglass white wine (optional)
$\frac{1}{2}$ pint stock (use $\frac{3}{4}$ pint if not using wine)
salt and pepper
bouquet garni
3 medium-size potatoes (quartered lengthways), or 8 small new potatoes (whole)
1 tablespoon parsley (chopped)

Method

Put the pork in a pan, cover with water and
simmer for 45 minutes; allow it to cool in the
liquid, then drain. Remove skin and cut into
lardons ($\frac{1}{4}$-inch thick strips, about $1\frac{1}{2}$ inches
long). Blanch the onions and drain.
Watchpoint If using the gammon rasher
remove the rind, cut into lardons and blanch
with the onions. Wash and trim the mushrooms, cut in half or quarters depending on
their size.

Trim the chops, brown in the butter in a
shallow pan, draw aside and remove from
the pan. Put the mushrooms, onions and
pork or bacon into the pan and sauté until
golden-brown. Then stir in the flour, add the
wine and stock and bring to the boil. Season,
replace the chops in the pan and add the
herbs. Cover and simmer on top of the stove
or in the oven at 350°F or Mark 4 for 20
minutes.

Meanwhile quarter the potatoes lengthways or leave whole, if new ones. Trim the
sharp edge of the quarters, blanch them and
add to the pan. Continue cooking for a
further 20 minutes, or until both meat and
potatoes are tender. Remove bouquet garni
and dish up chops and potatoes sprinkled
with chopped parsley. Serve with courgettes
au gratin.

Courgettes au gratin

Main course

1 lb courgettes
½ teaspoon salt
¼ pint water
1 egg
1 small carton (3 fl oz) double
　cream
2 rounded tablespoons Gruyère
　cheese (grated)
black pepper (ground from mill)
½ oz butter

Method

Wipe courgettes, trim the ends, cut in slanting ½-inch slices and put in a sauté pan with the salt and water. Cover pan and cook over moderate heat until water has almost evaporated.

Mix the egg, cream and cheese together, reserving 1 tablespoon of cheese, and season with black pepper.

Slide courgettes carefully into ovenproof gratin dish. Pour over the creamy mixture and sprinkle with the reserved cheese. Dot the top with shavings of butter and bake in oven at 400°F or Mark 6 for about 10 minutes or until just set and golden-brown.

Nusskuchen

4 oz butter
4 oz caster sugar
2 eggs
1½ oz ground hazelnuts (toasted) —
  see page 155
1 teaspoon instant coffee
1 tablespoon warm milk
4 oz self-raising flour
pinch of salt

For filling
1 lb dessert apples (Cox's orange
  pippin variety) - peeled, cored and
  sliced
2 tablespoons apricot jam
grated rind and juice of ½ lemon

To decorate
icing sugar (for dusting), or 2 oz
  plain chocolate (melted)

8-inch diameter sandwich tin

Method
Grease and flour the tin; set
oven at 375°F or Mark 5.

Soften the butter in a bowl,
add the sugar and work until
light and fluffy. Separate the
eggs and beat the yolks into the
butter and sugar. Stir in the prepared nuts. Dissolve the coffee
in the warm milk; sift the flour
with the salt and whisk the egg
whites until stiff.

Fold the flour into the mixture
with the coffee-flavoured milk,
then fold in the egg whites. Turn
mixture into the prepared tin and
bake in pre-set oven for about
25 minutes until cake is firm to
the touch and has shrunk slightly
from the sides of the tin. Turn
on to a rack to cool.

Meanwhile peel, core and
slice the apples and place in a
shallow pan with the jam, lemon rind and juice. Cover and
cook until apples are soft; leave
to cool.

Split the cake in half and fill
with the cooled apple mixture.
Finish with a dusting of icing
sugar or spread with the melted
chocolate, using a palette knife.

Appendix

Notes and basic recipes

Anchovy butter

Soften 2 oz unsalted butter on a plate with a palette knife, crush or pound 5-6 anchovy fillets (previously soaked in milk to remove excess salt), and add these to the butter with black pepper ground from the mill, together with 2 teaspoons anchovy essence to strengthen the flavour and give a delicate pink colour.

Aspic jelly

This is a jelly made from good fish, chicken, or meat stock very slightly sharpened with wine and a few drops of wine vinegar. Care must be taken that the stock is well flavoured and seasoned and that it is not too sharp, only pleasantly acidulated.

With certain delicately flavoured foods, such as fish, eggs or prawns, home-made aspic adds to and enhances the flavour. If you need aspic for brushing over sliced meat, use the commercially prepared variety, which is excellent for this - especially if a small quantity of the water is replaced by sherry. Make up according to directions on the packet or can.

Aspic, and most jellies containing wine, will keep for several days in the refrigerator. To do this, pour the liquid aspic into a jug, leave to set, then pour about ½ inch cold water over the top, and refrigerate. Remember to pour water off before melting the aspic for use.

Aspic jelly

Basic recipe
2½ fl oz sherry
2½ fl oz white wine
2 oz gelatine
1¾ pints cold stock
1 teaspoon wine vinegar
2 egg whites

Method

Add wines to gelatine and set aside. Pour cold stock into scalded pan, add vinegar. Whisk egg whites to a froth, add them to the pan, set over moderate heat and whisk backwards and downwards until the stock is hot. Then add gelatine, which by now will have absorbed the wine, and continue whisking steadily until boiling point has been reached.

Stop whisking and allow liquid to rise to the top of the pan ; turn off heat or draw pan aside and leave to settle for about 5 minutes, then bring it again to the boil, draw pan aside once more and leave liquid to settle. At this point the liquid should look clear ; if not, repeat the boiling-up process.

Filter the jelly through a cloth or jelly bag.

The aspic should be allowed to cool before use.

The stock for aspic jelly may be white (chicken or veal), brown (beef) or fish, according to the dish being made.

Béchamel sauce

Using the quantities given in the particular recipe, put the onion and spices in the milk and heat gently, without boiling, in a covered saucepan for 5-7 minutes.

Pour off into a jug and wipe out the pan. Melt the butter in this, and stir in the flour off the heat. Strain in a good third of the milk, blend and add remaining milk. When thoroughly mixed, season lightly, return to the heat and stir continually until boiling. Boil for 2-3 minutes, then adjust the seasoning.

Breadcrumbs

To make crumbs : take a large loaf (the best type to use is a sandwich loaf) at least two days old. Cut off the crust and keep to one side. Break up bread into crumbs either by rubbing through a wire sieve or a Mouli sieve, or by working in an electric blender.

Spread crumbs on to a sheet of paper laid on a baking tin and cover with another sheet of paper to keep off any dust. Leave to dry in a warm temperature - the plate rack, or warming drawer, or the top of the oven, or even the airing cupboard, is ideal. The crumbs may take a day or two to dry thoroughly, and they must be crisp before storing in a jar. To make them uniformly fine, sift them through a wire bowl strainer.

To make browned crumbs : bake the crusts in a slow oven until golden-brown, then crush or grind through a mincer. Sift and store as for white crumbs. These browned ones are known as raspings and are used for any dish that is coated with a sauce and browned in the oven.

Chicken stock

This should ideally be made from the giblets (neck, gizzard, heart and feet, if available), but never the liver which imparts a bitter flavour. This is better kept for making pâté, or sautéd and used as a savoury. Dry fry the giblets with an onion, washed but not peeled, and cut in half. To dry fry, use a thick pan with a lid, with barely enough fat to cover the bottom. Allow the pan to get very hot before putting in the giblets and onion, cook on full heat until lightly coloured. Remove pan from heat before covering with 2 pints of cold water. Add a large pinch of salt, a few peppercorns and a bouquet garni (bayleaf, thyme, parsley) and simmer gently for 1-2

hours. Alternatively, make the stock when you cook the chicken by putting the giblets in the roasting tin around the chicken with the onion and herbs, and use the measured quantity of water. This is preferable to bouillon cube stock for, in reducing the liquid with bouillon, there is the danger of the finished sauce being too salty.

Deep fat frying

Choose a deep heavy gauge pan (fat bath or deep fryer) which covers source of heat, complete with a wire basket to fit. Or buy a separate folding wire basket for fitting into any saucepan (which must, however, be of reasonably heavy gauge because fat is heated to high temperatures in deep fat frying). This separate basket is useful when only occasionally deep fat frying because its flexibility means it can be used in an ordinary frying pan for cooking small foods such as croûtons.

When frying foods coated in soft batter mixture, you may find it easier to fry them in a fat bath without using a wire basket since batter tends to stick to the basket.

Suitable fats to use are : vegetable or nut oil ; lard clarified dripping or commercially prepared fat, but it is better not to mix these. Olive oil and margarine are not suitable for deep frying. Never fill pan with more than one-third fat or oil.

Melt the fat, or put the oil, over moderate heat, then increase heat until right cooking temperature is reached. Oil must never be heated above 375°F, and for sunflower oil, and some commercially prepared fats (eg, Spry, Cookeen) 360°F is the highest recommended temperature. It is important to remember that oil does not 'haze as solid fats do, until heated to a much higher temperature than is required — or is safe — for frying.

Apart from food cooked on a rising temperature (eg. pirozhki), the fat or oil should never be below 340°F, as it is essential that the surface of the food is sealed immediately. This means it does not absorb fat, and is more digestible.

The best way of testing temperature is with a frying thermometer. Before using, it should be stood in a pan of hot water then carefully dried before putting into the fat bath. The hot water warms the glass so that it does not break when plunged into the hot fat.

If you have no thermometer, drop in a small piece of the food to be cooked (eg. a chip). If the fat or oil is at the right temperature, the food will rise immediately to the top and bubbles appear round it. Afternatively drop in a cube of day-old bread, which should turn golden-brown in 20 seconds at 375°F; 60 seconds at 360°F.

French dressing

Mix 1 tablespoon wine, or tarragon, vinegar with $\frac{1}{2}$ teaspoon each of salt and freshly ground black pepper. Add 3 tablespoons of salad oil.

When dressing thickens, taste for correct seasoning; if it is sharp yet oily, add more salt. Quantities should be in the ratio of 1 part vinegar to 3 parts oil.

For **vinaigrette dressing,** add freshly chopped herbs of choice.

Fritter batter

4 tablespoons plain flour
pinch of salt
2 egg yolks
1 tablespoon melted butter, or oil
$\frac{1}{4}$ pint milk
1 egg white

Method
Sift flour with salt into a bowl, make a well in centre of flour, add egg yolks, melted butter, or oil, and mix with milk to a smooth batter; beat thoroughly. Stand in a cool place for 30 minutes. Just before frying, whisk egg white stiffly, fold into batter. Fry in deep fat or up to $\frac{1}{2}$-inch depth for shallow frying.

Gelatine

As gelatine setting strength varies according to brand, it is essentiel to follow instructions given on the pack. For instance. Davis gelatine recommend 1 oz to set 2 pints of liquid.

Glacé icing

4-5 tablespoons granulated sugar
$\frac{1}{4}$ pint water
8-12 oz icing sugar (finely sifted)
flavouring essence and colouring
(as required)

Method
Make sugar syrup by dissolving sugar in $\frac{1}{4}$ pint of water in a small saucepan. Bring to the boil, and boil steadily for 10 minutes. Remove pan from the heat and when quite cold, add the icing sugar, tablespoon at a time, and beat thoroughly with a wooden spatula. The icing should coat back of spoon and look very glossy. Warm the pan gently on a very low heat.

Watchpoint The pan must not get too hot. You should be able to touch the bottom with the palm of your hand.

Flavour and colour icing; spread over cake with palette knife.

Ice cream — methods of freezing

Refrigerator or home-freezer Use the ice trays of a refrigerator or a stainless steel bowl in a home-freezer.

Churn freezer This type can be manual or electric. The former is more generally used, and it consists of a wooden bucket with a metal container fitted with a dasher. The bucket is first packed with a mixture of three parts ice to one part salt, in layers, and the ice-cream mixture is poured into the container. A handle is then turned which revolves the dasher, and so not only gradually scrapes away the mixture from round the sides as it freezes, but also churns, or beats, it at the same time.

The electric churn machines, of which there are two types, operate on the same principle. One type is set in the ice-making compartment of the refrigerator (so that there is no necessity for extra ice), with the flex leading to an electric plug outside the refrigerator. The other variety requires a quantity of ice.

The mixture to be frozen must not come more than half to three-quarters of the way up the sides of the container.

To obtain a low freezing temperature a mixture of ice and salt is used. The salt should be coarse rock salt (known as freezing salt), obtainable from some fishmongers and from big stores. The ice is best chipped off from a block rather than ice made by an ice-maker.

Watchpoint The pieces of ice should not be so large that the salt trickles through the gaps between them, as would certainly happen if ice cubes from the refrigerator were used. This can be prevented if the pieces are well jabbed down with the ice pick when filling them into the bucket. After packing with ice and salt, leave the churn for 2-3 minutes before starting to turn the handle.

How to churn

Start by turning the handle smoothly and evenly for about 3 minutes. Then leave for a further 3-4 minutes. Test the handle again, and if it shows any resistance continue to churn until the handle is really stiff to turn round. If the mixture is made with the right proportion of sugar, the time for churning should not exceed 5-6 minutes. When ice is stiff, pour off any water from the hole in the side of the bucket, remove dasher and push mixture down from around sides into bottom of container.

Cover the top with foil or double greaseproof paper and replace the lid. Refill the churn with ice and salt, stop up the hole in the lid, cover with sacking or similar cloth and leave for at least 1 hour.

Lemon jelly

1¾ oz gelatine
1½ pints water
pared rind of 3 lemons
7½ fl oz lemon juice
2 sticks of cinnamon
7 oz lump sugar
whites and shells (wiped and lightly crushed) of 2 eggs
2½ fl oz sherry, or water

This basic recipe makes 2 pints of lemon jelly. Lemon jelly is used as a clear sweet jelly in many desserts.

Method

Soak gelatine in ½ pint of the water. Pour remaining 1¼ pints of water into a scalded pan, add the lemon rind and juice, cinnamon and sugar ; warm over gentle heat until sugar is dissolved.

Whip egg whites to a froth, add to the pan with the shells, gelatine and sherry (or water).

Whisk backwards and downwards until liquid reaches boiling point. Allow the liquid to boil up three times, drawing pan aside between each boiling to allow it to settle.

Have ready the scalded jelly bag with a bowl underneath and turn the contents of the pan into it. Once the jelly begins to run through, take up the bowl (placing another one underneath) and pour it back into bag. After a few times jelly running through should be crystal clear. Then allow it to run through completely before moving bag or bowl. A screwtop jar or jug of hot water placed in the bag helps to keep the jelly liquid.

Macaroons (almond)

7 oz caster sugar
1 oz granulated sugar
4 oz ground almonds
$\frac{1}{2}$ oz rice flour
2-3 egg whites (according to size)
2-3 drops of vanilla essence
rice paper
split almonds

This makes approximately 9.

Method
Set oven at 350°F or Mark 4.

Mix the sugars, ground almonds and rice flour together in a mixing bowl; add the egg whites and the essence and beat all together with a wooden spoon for about 5 minutes. Scrape down sides of bowl; allow to stand for 5 minutes.

Meanwhile cut the rice paper into 3-inch squares and place, shiny side down, on a dry baking sheet. Continue beating the almond mixture for 5 minutes more until thick and white. Using a bag and $\frac{1}{2}$-inch

pipe, shape neatly on to rice paper squares, place a split almond in the centre of each macaroon and bake in pre-set oven for 20-30 minutes.

Mayonnaise

2 egg yolks
salt and pepper
dry mustard
$\frac{1}{4}$ cup of salad oil
2 tablespoons wine vinegar

This recipe will make $\frac{1}{2}$ pint of mayonnaise.

Method
Work egg yolks and seasonings with a small whisk or wooden spoon in a bowl until thick ; then start adding the oil drop by drop. When 2 tablespoons of oil have been added this mixture will be very thick. Now carefully stir in 1 teaspoon of the vinegar.

The remaining oil can then be added a little more quickly, either 1 tablespoon at a time and beaten thoroughly between each addition until it is absorbed, or in a thin steady stream if you are using an electric beater.

When all the oil has been absorbed, add remaining vinegar to taste, and extra salt and pepper as necessary.

To thin and lighten mayonnaise add a little hot water. For a coating consistency, thin with a little cream or milk.

Eggs should not come straight from the refrigerator. If oil is cloudy or chilled, it can be slightly warmed which will lessen the chances of eggs curdling. Put oil bottle in a pan of hot water for a short time.

Watchpoint Great care must be taken to prevent mayonnaise curdling. Add oil drop by drop at first, and then continue adding it very slowly.

If mayonnaise curdles, start with a fresh yolk in another bowl and work well with seasoning, then add the curdled mixture to it very slowly and carefully. When curdled mixture is completely incorporated, more oil can be added if the mixture is too thin.

Nuts

To brown hazelnuts (already shelled): do not blanch first but bake for 7-8 minutes in a moderate oven at 350°F or Mark 4, then rub briskly in a rough cloth to remove skin. To grind, either chrop very finely or grind in a Mouli grater.

Almonds : buy them with their skins on. This way they retain their oil better. Blanching to remove the skins gives extra juiciness.

To blanch almonds : pour boiling water over the shelled nuts, cover the pan and leave until cool. Then the skins can be easily removed (test one with finger and thumb). Drain, rinse in cold water and press skins off with fingers. Rinse, dry thoroughly.

To brown blanched almonds : bake as for hazelnuts (above).

To chop almonds : first blanch, skin, chop and then brown them in the oven, if desired.

To shred almonds : first blanch, skin, split in two and cut each half lengthways in fine pieces. These can then be used as they are or browned quickly in the oven, with or without a sprinkling of caster sugar.

To flake almonds : first blanch, skin, and cut horizontally into flakes with a small sharp knife.

To grind almonds : first blanch, skin, chop and pound into a paste (use a pestle and mortar, or a grinder, or the butt end of a rolling pin). Home-prepared ground almonds taste much better than the ready-ground variety.

Pistachios : treat as for almonds, but when blanching add a pinch of bicarbonate of soda to the water to preserve the colour.

Poaching fruit

The most important point to remember when cooking fruit is that the water and sugar should first be made into a syrup. An average proportion for this syrup is 3 rounded tablespoons granulated sugar to $\frac{1}{2}$ pint water per lb of fruit. Heat gently in a pan to dissolve sugar, boil rapidly for 2 minutes before the fruit is added. The syrup may be flavoured with pared lemon rind or a vanilla pod.

Prepare fruit as directed in recipe, then place rounded side down in a pan with syrup and bring very slowly to boil. Allow syrup to boil up and over fruit and then reduce heat, cover pan and leave to simmer very gently until tender.

Even fully ripe fruit must be thoroughly cooked to allow the syrup to penetrate, sweeten and prevent discolouration.

Praline powder

To make praline powder heat almonds and sugar gently in a small heavy pan. When sugar is a liquid caramel, stir carefully with a metal spoon to toast nuts on all sides. Turn on to an oiled tin and leave to set. When cold, crush praline with a rolling pin or put through a nut-mill, mincer or grater.

Redcurrant jelly

It is not possible to give a specific quantity of redcurrants as the recipe is governed by the amount of juice made, which is variable.

Method

Wash the fruit and, without removing from the stems, put in a 7 lb jam jar or stone crock. Cover and stand in deep pan of hot water. Simmer on top of the stove or in the oven at 350°F or Mark 4, mashing the fruit a little from time to time, until all the juice is extracted (about 1 hour).

Then turn fruit into a jelly-bag, or double linen strainer, and allow to drain undisturbed overnight over a basin.

Watchpoint To keep the jelly clear and sparkling, do not try to speed up the draining process by forcing juice through; this will only make the jelly cloudy.

Now measure juice. Allowing 1 lb lump, or preserving sugar, to each pint of juice, mix juice and sugar together, dissolving over slow heat. When dissolved, bring to the boil, boil hard for 3-5 minutes and skim with a wooden spoon. Test a little on a saucer allow jelly to cool, tilt saucer and, if jelly is set, it will wrinkle. Put into jam jars, place small circles of greaseproof paper over jelly, label and cover with jam pot covers. Store in a dry larder until required.

Redcurrant jelly glaze

Home-made redcurrant jelly is best as it gives the right sharpness of flavour to the fresh fruit. Beat the jelly with a fork or small whisk until it liquefies, then rub through a strainer into a small saucepan. Heat gently without stirring until quite clear (boiling will spoil both colour and flavour). When brushing this glaze over the fruit use a very soft brush. Always work from the centre outwards, drawing the brush, well laden with the glaze, towards the edge.

Rich shortcrust pastry

8 oz plain flour
pinch of salt
6 oz butter
1 rounded dessertspoon caster sugar (for sweet pastry)
1 egg yolk
2-3 tablespoons cold water

Method

Sift the flour with a pinch of salt into a mixing bowl. Drop in the butter and cut it into the flour until the small pieces are well coated, then rub them in with the fingertips until the mixture looks like fine breadcrumbs. Stir in the sugar, mix egg yolk with water, tip into the fat and flour and mix quickly with a palette knife to a firm dough.

Turn on to a floured board and knead lightly until smooth. If possible, chill in refrigerator (wrapped in greaseproof paper, a polythene bag, or foil) for 30 minutes before using.

Tomatoes, skinning and seeding

Scald and skin tomatoes by placing them in a bowl, pouring boiling water over them, counting 12 before pouring off the hot water and replacing it with cold. The skin then comes off easily. To remove seeds, cut a slice from the top (not stalk end) of each tomato, reserve slices; hold tomato in hollow of your palm, flick out seeds with the handle of a teaspoon, using the bowl of the spoon to detach the core. So much the better if the spoon is worn and therefore slightly sharp.

Glossary

Bain-marie (au) To cook at temperature just below boiling point in a saucepan standing in a larger pan of simmering water. May be carried out in oven or on top of stove.

Baking blind Pre-cooking a pastry case before filling. Chill pastry case, line with crumpled greaseproof paper and three-parts fill with uncooked rice or beans. An 8-inch diameter flan ring holding a 6-8 oz quantity of pastry should cook for about 26 minutes in an oven at 400°F or Mark 6. Take out paper and beans for last 5 minutes baking.

Blanch To whiten meats and remove strong tastes from vegetables by bringing to boil from cold water and draining before further cooking. Green vegetables should be put into boiling water and cooked for up to 1 minute.

Caramelise 1 To dissolve sugar slowly in water then boil steadily, without stirring, to a toffee-brown colour. 2 To give a thin caramel topping by dusting top of sweet with caster or icing sugar, and grilling slowly.

Clarified butter Butter cleared by heating gently until foaming, skimming well, pouring off clear yellow oil, leaving sediment (milk solids) in pan.

Court bouillon Stock made from water, root vegetables, wine or vinegar, seasoning, herbs for poaching fish or veal and for use in sauces.

Deglaze To heat stock and / or wine together with flavoursome sediments left in roasting / frying pan so that gravy / sauce is formed. (Remove excess fat first.)

Infuse To steep in liquid (not always boiling) in warm place to draw flavour into the liquid.

Julienne strip Strip of vegetable / meat cut to about $\frac{1}{8}$ inch by $1\frac{1}{2}$-2 inches long.

Lardons Small $\frac{1}{4}$-inch thick strips of fat about $1\frac{1}{2}$ inches long, cut from piece of larding bacon which is solid fat. They are used to give extra fat to cuts of meat that have little or none of their own to protect them from drying out during cooking. These strips are larded or sewn into the meat with a larding needle.

Liaison Mixture for thickening / binding sauce / gravy / soup. eg. roux, egg yolks, cream, kneaded butter (i.e. butter and flour in the ratio 2 to 1, kneaded together to a paste).

Marinate To soak raw meat / game / fish in cooked or raw spiced liquid (marinade) of wine, oil, herbs and vegetables for hours / days before cooking.

Panade Basic thickening for fish / meat / vegetable creams made from soaked crumbs, choux paste, or thick béchamel.

Poussin Baby chicken, 4-6 weeks old.

Refresh To pour cold water over previously blanched and drained food.

Sauté To brown food in butter, or oil and butter. Sometimes cooking is completed in a 'small' sauce - ie. one made on the food in the sauté pan.

Seasoned flour Flour to which salt and pepper have been added.

Shortening Fat which when worked into flour gives a 'short' crisp quality to pastry / cakes. Fats with least liquid, eg. lard, vegetable fat, contain most shortening power.

Soubise Denotes a purée of onions, usually mixed with rice, seasonings, butter and cream, or with a bechamel sauce instead of the rice.

Sprue A thinner variety of asparagus.

Stock Liquid or jelly made by simmering meat / bones / vegetables / fish for several hours. Used for making gravy / sauce / soup. (See also Chicken stock, page 151.)

Syrup 1 Sugar and water boiled together to the specified temperature. Used for stewing fruit, adding to fresh fruit salad, crystallising fruit. 2 Liquid derived from sugar cane : treacle or golden syrup. 3 Stock : 8 oz granulated or lump sugar dissolved in $\frac{3}{4}$ pint water over gentle heat, brought to boil and boiled for 10 minutes. Used for mixing with icing to give it a glossy appearance.

Velouté Describes soups or sauces of a velvety consistency, made by passing a well flavoured stock on to a bland roux.

Index